WJEC B Religious Studies
Religion & Human Experience

Laura Burridge • Tanya Hill • David Sharpe

Series Editor: Chris Owens

Heinemann is an imprint of Pearson Education Limited, a company incorporated in England and Wales, having its registered office at Edinburgh Gate, Harlow, Essex, CM20 2JE. Registered company number: 872828

www.pearsonschoolsandfecolleges.co.uk

Heinemann is a registered trademark of Pearson Education Ltd

Text © Pearson Education Limited, 2009

First published 2009

13
10 9 8 7 6 5

British Library Cataloguing in Publication Data is available from the British Library on request.

10-digit ISBN 0435501607
13-digit ISBN 978 0 435 50160 0

Edited by Florence Production Ltd, Stoodleigh, Devon
Reviewed by Graham Davies
Developed by Sandra Stafford
Designed by Wooden Ark Studios
Typeset by 𝐓 Tek-Art, Crawley Down, West Sussex
Produced by Florence Production Ltd, Stoodleigh, Devon
Original illustrations © Pearson Education Limited 2009
Illustrated by Ben Swift
Cover design by Pearson Education Ltd
Picture research by Suzi Paz
Cover photo © Marcus Spedding/iStockPhotos
Printed in Malaysia, CTP-KHL

Acknowledgements

The authors and publisher would like to thank the following individuals and organisations for permission to reproduce photographs:

GoldMund/iStockPhoto p. 13. North Wind Picture Archives/Alamy p. 15. Peace Tax Campaign p. 18. Andrew Penner/iStockPhoto p. 20. Kathy Konkle/iStockPhoto p. 23. Mansell/Mansell/Time & Life Pictures/Getty Images p. 24. Artist unknown/Australian War Memorial p. 28. Artist unknown p. 28. Daniel Deme/epa/Corbis p. 28. Mary Evans Picture Library/Alamy p. 30. AFP/Getty Images p. 33. Gianni Muratore/Alamy p. 33. The London Art Archive/Alamy p. 34. www.pregnantpause.org p. 39. Cut2White p. 41. ROSLIN ROSLIN INSTITUTE/PA Photos p. 48. Nathan Watkins/iStockPhoto p. 52. Used with the permission of Gary Varvel and Creators Syndicate. All rights reserved p. 52. fabpics/Alamy p. 57. Tŷ Hafan. Registered charity: 1047912 p. 57. Pearson Education Ltd. 2007/Jules Selmes p. 57. It'sTime.ca p. 58. Joan Loitz/iStockPhoto p. 60. Coaster/Alamy p. 67. Christian Aid p. 69. Tzedek p. 69. HinduAID p. 69. Lebrecht Music and Arts Photo Library/Alamy p. 74. World Religions Photo Library/Alamy p. 74. Classic Image/Alamy p. 74. Tim Graham/Alamy p. 76. Jenny Speckels/iStockPhoto p. 80. Steven Wynn/iStockPhoto p. 82. Alex Bowie/Getty Images p. 96. Kathy Konkle/iStockPhoto p. 99. JamesBennet/iStockPhoto p. 102. Pearson Education Ltd. 2004/Debbie Rowe p. 112.

All Bible verses are taken from the **New Revised Standard Version Bible**, copyright © 1989 National Council of the Churches of Christ in the United States of America. Used by permission. All rights reserved. All verses from the Qur'an are used with permission of IPCI – Islamic Vision, Birmingham, UK.

We would like to thank the following people for permission to reproduce copyrighted material: Pages 56/57 National Association of Hospice Fundraisers from What is a Hospice, http://www.nahf.org.uk/metadot/index.pl?id=17868&isa=Category&op=show. Page 25 IPCI – Islamic Vision, Birmingham, UK. Page 25 Scripture taken from the HOLY BIBLE, NEW INTERNATIONAL VERSION®. Copyright © 1973, 1978, 1984 International Bible Society. Used by permission of Zondervan. All rights reserved.

Every effort has been made to contact copyright holders of material reproduced in this book. Any omissions will be rectified in subsequent printings if notice is given to the publishers.

Websites
The websites used in this material were correct and up to date at the time of publication. It is essential for tutors to preview each website before using it in class so as to ensure that the URL is still accurate, relevant and appropriate. We suggest that tutors bookmark useful websites and consider enabling students to access them through the school/college intranet.

Contents

Introduction

A note for teachers

This student book has been written especially to support the WJEC Religious Studies Specification B, Unit 2: *Religion and human experience* (full and short course). It covers the six main religions of the specification (Buddhism, Christianity, Hinduism, Islam, Judaism and Sikhism) and is part of an overall series comprising:

■ a first student book covering Unit 1 of the specification (*Religion and life issues*)
■ a teacher guide covering both units, and
■ an Active Teach CD-ROM containing support materials for both students and teachers.

The specification provides an ideal opportunity to gain a qualification in Religious Studies while studying a thematic course that looks in detail at some of the fascinating central questions and issues in human life and experience. The material covers the relevance of religious beliefs, practices, values and traditions related to these questions.

This book has been carefully based on the WJEC specification content, and develops approaches to learning and teaching that promote both engagement and enjoyment with challenge and support.

The authors

The authors of this student book all have active teaching and examining experience in England and Wales. This means they understand the demands of the specification and have, therefore, sensitively compiled a book to meet the requirements of students taking the course.

With the development of a new specification came the distinct need for a student book to explain the significant changes and provide a coherent and structured guide to the course. The result is this student book, which offers a comprehensive structure to following the course as well as providing information, lesson ideas and activities along with clear teaching and learning objectives for all teachers (including non-specialists).

Usefully, this book can also be used by students following GCSE Religious Studies courses for other boards, although students should check their course specifications with their teacher.

Purpose of the specification

WJEC Religious Studies Specification B, Unit 2: *Religion and human experience* offers a contemporary and modern approach to the study of religious education. It is different and distinct from many other examination board specifications, as it supports the use of a full page of visual stimuli for each question in the examination. The rationale here is that this helps students to identify with the issues involved and encourages them to be inspired, moved and changed by following a broad, satisfying and worthwhile course of study that challenges them and equips them to lead constructive lives in the modern world. The promotion of community cohesion is at the heart of this course.

Changes to the specification

The specification has changed dramatically according to the changing nature of education and the need to meet the demands of the world for students. The main changes that teachers *and* students should be aware of include the following.

■ There has been a reduction in the number of topics to four (Topic 1: Religion and conflict; Topic 2: Religion and medicine; Topic 3: Religious expression; Topic 4: Authority – Religion & State), along with a change of content in those topics. The reduction is the result of new Assessment Objectives (AOs), with a 50 per cent focus now given to AO1 (Describe, explain and analyse, using knowledge and understanding) and a 50 per cent focus to AO2 (Use evidence and reasoned argument to express and evaluate personal responses, informed insights and differing viewpoints). There is more information on this on pages 9–11.
■ There have been changes to the key concepts and key words in each topic.

- Level descriptor grids have been changed to a new range of 0 to 8 marks for extended questions.
- QWC (Quality of Written Communication) is now only assessed in the (e) questions of the extended writing sections.
- There have been changes to the style of the questions on the examination paper – for example, the 'state' questions have been removed and more emphasis has been given to extended writing answers (with more space for answers dedicated to these on the exam paper).
- There is an increased focus on learning *from* religion rather than simply learning *about* religion, and explicit reference to religious beliefs is now required in all extended written answers.
- 'Religious believers' is the new term used in examination questions when focusing on religous ideas.

Notes for teachers and students

Aims of this book

From the beginning to the end, this book provides a relevant, practical and comprehensive guide to this course. It supports both teachers and students in their study of the four topics from first looking at them through to revision and the examination. This resource allows students to develop their knowledge and understanding of the religions studied. It also gives them the opportunity to consider many current and important issues from religious and non-religious perspectives.

Skills are a vital element in any GCSE course, and this book will provide invaluable assistance to students in:

- developing skills when considering religious and other responses to moral, ethical and philosophical issues
- identifying, investigating and responding to fundamental questions of life and living.

Examination focus of the book

This book gives advice on general revision and how to prepare for the examination.

The **Grade Studio** features that appear throughout, and at the end of, each topic (see later for more details) give students guidance on the level descriptors used in the exam and how to write good answers.

The **Exam Café** feature on pages 116–123 works step by step through exam preparation. In an easily digestible format, it offers practical, yet realistic, advice about revising.

Religion and human experience has been written specifically to provide coverage of the key ideas and issues involved in the specification. It is designed to:

- be informative yet accessible to all students
- provide invaluable support throughout the course study.

What's in this book

This student book, which works in conjunction with the WJEC Religious Studies Specification B, Unit 2: *Religion and human experience*, has the following sections:

- the **introduction**, which you are reading now
- the **four topics** covered in the specification (Topic 1: Religion and conflict; Topic 2: Religion and medicine; Topic 3: Religious expression; Topic 4: Authority – Religion & State)
- **Exam Café** – an invaluable resource for students studying for their GCSE in Religious Studies
- **Glossary** – a reference tool for key terms and words used throughout the book.

Each of the above is covered in more detail in the text that follows.

The four topics

Each topic contains:

- a topic scene-setter (**The Big Picture**)
- a look at the key questions raised by the topic, and the key words and issues associated with those questions (**Develop Your Knowledge**)
- nine two-page spreads covering the **main topic content**
- two pages of different-level questions to check understanding of the topic material (**Remember and Reflect**)
- exam-style questions with level indicators, examiner's comments and model answers (**Grade Studio**).

These features, which are explained more fully in the following pages, have been carefully planned and designed to draw together the WJEC specification in a manageable and convenient way.

The Big Picture

This provides an overview of the topic. It explains to students what they will be studying (the content), why they are studying it (the rationale) and how they will study it (the approaches, activities and tasks). It also includes a 'Get started' activity, often linked to a picture or visual stimulus, that presents a task designed to engage students in the issues of the topic and give them some idea of the content to be studied.

Develop Your Knowledge

This lists the key information, key words and key questions of the topic. At a glance, it allows students to grasp the basic elements of knowledge they will gain in the study of the topic. It is also a useful reference point for reflection and checking information as it is studied.

Main topic content

The main content of each topic is covered in nine two-page spreads. Each spread equates to roughly one lesson of work – although teachers will need to judge for themselves if some of these need more time.

Each spread begins with the learning outcomes, so that students are aware of the focus and aims of the lesson. It then poses a leading question, often in connection with a visual stimulus, which encourages students to think quickly in general terms about the specific issues they will cover.

The text then attempts to answer, through a balanced viewpoint, one or two of the key questions raised in **Develop Your Knowledge**. The text carefully covers the views of both religious believers and non-believers. It is also punctuated with activities that range from simple tasks that can take place in the classroom to more complex tasks that can be tackled away from school.

A range of margin features adds extra depth and support to the main text for both students and the teacher.

- 'For debate' invites students to examine two sides of a controversial issue.
- 'Must think about!' directs students towards a key idea that they should consider.
- 'Sacred text' provides an extract from one of the religions covered in the topic to help students understand religious ideas and teachings.
- 'Research note' provides specific guidance about how students can research for themselves a particular issue/person/idea or event.

Remember and Reflect

This provides an opportunity for students to reflect on what they have learned and identify possible weaknesses or gaps in their knowledge. It also helps them to recognise key ideas in the specification content. Once students have tested their knowledge with the first set of questions, a cross-reference takes them back to the relevant part of the text so they can check their answers. A second set of questions helps them to develop the skills necessary for the examination.

Grade Studio

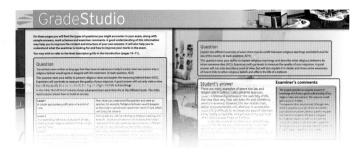

Grade Studio features in two ways throughout each topic:

- it appears occasionally through the main spreads as an extra consideration in relation to the lesson studied
- it appears as a two-page spread at the end of each topic with a range of different-level student answers and comments on these.

It helps students to become familiar with the level descriptors for both Assessment Objectives 1 and 2 (AO1 and AO2), and provides an explicit focus on how students can improve their answers using building skills and techniques. It has practice questions built in to give students some idea about the style of examination questions and how to write good answers in response to them. (More information on the level descriptors and AO1/AO2 grids can be found on pages 9–11.)

Exam Café

This feature has been specially designed to support students as they prepare for and approach the examination. It provides realistic and practical guidance on how to plan revision effectively and monitor knowledge and understanding of each topic. Exam Café contains:

- useful and practical revision tips for students
- comments on how a student's overall performance can be improved
- a checklist for studying each topic
- tasks that test revision strategies.

It is a motivating feature carefully put together to help engage students in effective revision, an aspect of the course that many students find difficult. As well as being an integral part of the student book, this feature is also available on the accompanying Active Teach CD-ROM.

Other resources in the series

Teacher guide

This guide essentially provides teachers with suggestions for teaching the whole of WJEC Religious Studies Specification B, Units 1 and 2.

Each topic in this guide contains ten spread-based lesson plans (one for **The Big Picture**, plus a further nine to correspond with the main content spreads in each student book). These plans give an exciting and engaging range of ideas and material that teachers can draw on to teach alongside or supplement the content of the student book. In addition, each lesson plan comes with either a supporting photocopiable worksheet or background notes on the three religions *not* covered in each topic.

Each lesson plan in the guide is meticulously cross-referenced to the corresponding materials in both student books. It also contains the lesson focus and learning outcomes as stated in the student books, then moves through a series of starter activities, development ideas, plenaries and homework/extension tasks. These have all been written to cover the student book lessons from as many angles as possible to help students think all the way round what are often sensitive and difficult issues that may well be outside their range of experience at this point in their lives.

The activities, discussions, ideas, debates and other ideas have all been designed and road-tested to inspire and motivate students to learn as thoroughly as possible the content of the specification.

Active Teach CD-ROM

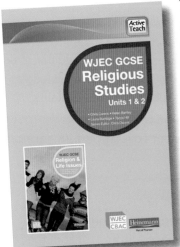

This is designed to support the materials in both student books and the Teacher's guide. It is a set of resources that will help to make lesson activities more interactive. These activities work best with an interactive whiteboard but could also be used individually on computers. The Active Teach CD-ROM also contains extra worksheets and pictures that can be used in the delivery of the course.

Student book 1 – Religion & Life Issues

The first student book accompanying the WJEC course, Specification B, Unit 1 takes a similar format to this student book but focuses on four different topics:

- Topic 1 Relationships
- Topic 2 Is it fair?
- Topic 3 Looking for meaning
- Topic 4 Our world.

About the exam

The WJEC GCSE Religious Studies Specification B, Unit 1 option is assessed by a written paper of 1 hour 45 minutes. This paper contains four main questions – one for each topic studied. Each question comprises five parts – **a**–**e**.

Students are required to answer all the questions on the paper. Writing lines are provided for them to write their responses, giving them some guidance on the expected length of their answers. The number of marks available for each question is clearly shown, and all questions follow a set format and style. Students' answers are marked using level descriptor grids (which can be found on pages 10–11). They are assessed according to the objectives.

- AO1: Describe, explain and analyse, using knowledge and understanding.
- AO2: Use evidence and reasoned argument to express and evaluate personal responses, informed insights and differing viewpoints.

AO1 and AO2 are weighted equally in the paper (50 per cent each) and are interrelated, which means students should show connections between ideas. Students need to be made aware of the differences between AO1 and AO2 and the style of questions in the examination.

The information that follows outlines the set structure of the questions, including the numbers of marks available and the focus of assessment for each question.

a These questions are always worth 2 marks; they use AO1 assessment, and the corresponding level descriptor grids are used to mark this type of response. These questions focus on key words and ideas. They look at what religious believers mean by using particular terms in relation to one of the key ideas within each topic of study – for example: *Explain what religious believers mean by the term* _____.

b These questions are always worth 4 marks; they use AO1 assessment, and the corresponding level descriptor grids are used to mark this type of response. The focus is on students showing their knowledge and understanding of how the beliefs of religious believers mean they act or view something in a particular way – for example: *Explain how having a religious faith may* _____.

c These questions are always worth 4 marks; they use AO2 assessment, and the corresponding level descriptor grids are used to mark this type of response. The focus is on students explaining why a religious believer would agree or disagree with a given statement of information – for example: *'Statement.' Give two reasons why a religious believer might agree or disagree with this statement.*

d These questions are always worth 6 marks; they use AO1 assessment, and the corresponding level descriptor grids are used to mark this type of response. The focus is on students showing knowledge and understanding about a key concept in two different religious traditions. Detail and explanation is required in their answers rather than simply description – for example: *Explain from two different religious traditions the teachings about* _____.

e These questions are always worth 8 marks; they use AO2 assessment, and the corresponding level descriptor grids are used to mark this type of response. The focus is on students giving their own views about some of the issues studied as well as showing their awareness of a range of other views and drawing on religious and moral knowledge to show the impact it might have on individuals and society. The question always begins with a statement that is the focus of the answer – for example: *'Statement.' Do you agree? Give reasons or evidence for your answer, showing that you have thought of more than one point of view. You must include reference to religious beliefs in your answer.*

Marking grids and level descriptors

AO1

The level descriptor grids show the development of answers up the scale. AO1 focuses on knowledge and understanding; the higher levels indicate that students need to be able to relate ideas together and be concise, detailed and thorough in their answers. There are four levels for each descriptor (apart from the 2 mark questions), and please note that, for the higher levels in the 6 mark questions, a range of marks is available.

2 mark questions (question a)

Level	Level descriptor	Mark total
0	No statement of relevant information or explanation.	0
1	A statement of information or explanation that is limited in scope or content.	1
2	An accurate and appropriate explanation of a central teaching, theme or concept.	2

4 mark questions (question b)

Level	Level descriptor	Mark total
0	Makes no link between beliefs and practices.	0
1	A simple link between beliefs and practices.	1
2	An explicit link between beliefs and practices. Limited use of specialist language.	2
3	Analysis showing some awareness and insight into religious facts, ideas, practices and explanations. Uses and interprets a range of religious language and terms.	3
4	Coherent analysis showing awareness and insight into religious facts, ideas, practices and explanations. Uses religious language and terms extensively and interprets them accurately.	4

6 mark questions (question d)

Level	Level descriptor	Mark total
0	A statement of information or explanation that has no relevant content.	0
1	A relevant statement of information or explanation that is limited in scope.	1
2	An accurate account of information or an appropriate explanation of a central teaching, theme or concept. Limited use of religious language.	2
3	An account or explanation indicating knowledge and understanding of key religious ideas, practices, explanations or concepts. Uses and interprets religious language in appropriate context.	3–4
4	A coherent account or explanation showing awareness and insight into religious facts, ideas, practices and explanations. Uses religious language and terms extensively and interprets them accurately.	5–6

AO2

The level descriptors show the development of answers up the scale. AO2 focuses on students explaining the reasoning behind different views and, more importantly, justifying their own opinions. The higher levels indicate that students need to be able to relate ideas together and be concise, detailed and thorough in their answers. There are four levels for each descriptor and please note that the higher levels in the 8 mark questions have more than 1 mark available.

4 mark questions (question c)

Level	Level descriptor	Mark total
0	Makes no relevant point of view.	0
1	A simple, appropriate justification of a point of view.	1
2	EITHER an expanded justification of one point of view, with appropriate example and/or illustration, which includes religious teaching OR two simple, appropriate justifications of a point of view.	2
3	An expanded justification of one point of view, with appropriate example and/or illustration, which includes religious teaching with a second simple appropriate justification of a point of view (which may be an alternative to the first).	3
4	An expanded justification of two viewpoints, incorporating the religious teaching and moral aspects at issue and their implications for the individual and the rest of society.	4

8 mark questions (question e)

Level	Level descriptor	Mark total
0	Makes no relevant point of view.	0
1	Communicates clearly and appropriately EITHER a simple justification of a point of view, possibly linked to evidence or example and making a simple connection between religion and people's lives OR two simple appropriate justifications of points of view.	1–2
2	Communicates clearly and appropriately using limited specialist language EITHER an expanded justification of one point of view, with appropriate example, which includes religious teaching and/or illustration, AND either a second simple appropriate justification OR two appropriate justifications of points of view linked to evidence or example, which includes religious teaching.	3–4
3	Communicates clearly and appropriately using and interpreting specialist language an expanded justification of one point of view, with appropriate examples, which includes religious teaching and/or illustration. There is also an adequate recognition of an alternative or different point of view.	5–6
4	Communicates clearly and appropriately using specialist language extensively a thorough discussion, including alternative or different views of the religious teachings and moral aspects at issue and their implications for the individual and the rest of society. Uses relevant evidence and religious/or moral reasoning to formulate judgement.	7–8

1 Religion and conflict

The Big Picture

- In this topic you will be addressing various ethical issues relating to religion and conflict.
- This topic covers three principal religions: Christianity, Islam and Buddhism.
- You will need to focus on at least two principal religions.

You will look at:

- religious practices and teachings about peace and conflict
- the nature and purpose of suffering and what support is available to help those who suffer
- religious teachings about forgiveness and reconciliation
- the range of different beliefs and practices that exist with regard to conflict and war, including pacifism
- attitudes to non-violent protest.

You will also think about the different attitudes that exist towards these ethics and practices.

What?

You will:

- develop your knowledge and understanding of issues of peace, reconciliation and conflict
- focus on peace, forgiveness and attitudes towards war
- explain how religious teachings can help us to understand forgiveness and reconciliation
- make links between these teachings and your own ideas and opinions.

Why?

Because:

- these questions and issues are central to an understanding of human life and experience
- these are major areas of discussion and are important in the development of local, national and international relations in today's world
- there are different sides to how people view these subjects
- it is impossible to live in 21st-century Britain and not encounter these issues.

How?

By:

- studying and recalling information about religious teachings on these issues
- exploring the relevance and practicality of religious beliefs, practices, values and traditions in the world today
- considering appropriate examples of religious charities/organisations and religious believers and how they work for peace
- reviewing evidence from various references and sources appropriate to these issues
- analysing others' points of view and comparing them to your own.

We want peace
by Lenny Kravitz

We're on the eve of destruction my friends

We are about to go to war
Politicians think that war is the way
But we know that love has the power

We want peace
We want it yes
We want peace
We want it yes
We want peace
And we want it fast

The solution is simple and plain
There won't be peace if we don't try
In a war there is nothing to gain
When so many people will die

Activities

1   Discuss the ideas the lyrics give about peace.

2   In no more than 20 words, write down what you
    believe is the meaning of peace.

3   Draw a picture or symbol that you believe
    represents peace.

Develop Your Knowledge

This topic is about religion and conflict. Read the information below, which will help you to think about the issues, before you begin more detailed work.

Key information

- Making peace can be difficult if there are differences of opinion or if people feel strongly about certain issues.
- All religious traditions have teachings about peace.
- Attempts to maintain peace have resulted in the formation of organisations and groups that work to achieve peace.
- Interfaith dialogue emphasises the need for different faith groups to work together and remove misunderstandings.
- People suffer in many different ways, for example through natural disasters, ill health or because of other people's actions.
- Suffering can be eased in many ways. Responding to those who suffer is at the heart of many religions.
- There are many religious teachings on forgiveness.
- The concept of 'forgiveness' varies from person to person and in each situation.
- War and conflict are facts of life and have been around from the earliest periods of history.
- A war should always be the last resort, once every method of resolving the situation has been explored.
- Various conditions and theories exist to say what constitutes a just war.
- There is a range of attitudes towards non-violent protest.

Key words

*conflict clashes and breakdowns of relationships

interfaith community a community that makes possible religious respect and dialogue between and among all people

*interfaith dialogue exploring common grounds between different faith groups

*just war a war undertaken to protect the innocent or those being violated and to restore justice and peace

moral evil suffering caused by other humans, for example the Holocaust

natural evil suffering not caused by someone or something, for example volcanic eruptions or a tsunami

*non-violent protest showing disapproval without damaging property or causing any threat

*pacifism the belief that any form of violence or war is unacceptable

*reconciliation bringing harmony to a situation of disagreement and discord

suffering patience, endurance: the bearing of (or undergoing) pain or distress

*We draw attention to these key words in particular because they are the ones that appear in the WJEC specification.

- How can peace be made and kept?
- How can good relationships be developed between people?
- How can communities work together?
- How can different religions support peace by talking to each other?
- Why do the innocent suffer?
- How can those suffering be helped?
- Is forgiveness possible?
- How important is forgiveness?
- How important is it to forgive?
- How do people learn to forgive?
- Is it ever right to fight?
- How can war/conflict be avoided?
- Can a war ever be 'just'?
- How can non-violent protest be used?

For interest

Did you know?

- The shortest war on record took place in 1896, when Zanzibar surrendered to Britain after 38 minutes.
- The longest was the so-called Hundred Years War between Britain and France. It actually lasted 116 years, ending in 1453.
- In 1998, the United States spent more than $35 billion on its nuclear war programme.

Adapted from www.didyouknow.org/ fastfacts/war.htm

Important questions

- A large number of history's wars have been fought in the name of religion. Whose side is God on?
- Do you think there will ever be peace in the world?
- Why do we need nuclear weapons? Are they a cause or a preventative of war?

1.1 Peace (1)

The next two pages will help you to:

- explore issues of peace, how peace is agreed and how it is kept
- debate whether religion helps to maintain peace.

- Have you ever had to make peace between people? Perhaps a group of friends or family?

How can peace be made and kept?

It could be argued that, in order to make and keep peace, disagreement and conflict must be avoided. This can often be difficult if there are differences of opinion or if people feel strongly about certain issues. Differences in personality can often result in conflict. Many arguments and disagreements begin because people feel that they 'can't get along'.

Activities

1 **a** Make a list of the last three arguments that you can remember having. What were the arguments about?

   b Discuss your answers with the class. Have they had similar disagreements?

2 **a** Read the list below about ways to achieve peace.
   - Attend a peace rally.
   - Get to know your neighbours.
   - Make friends with someone of another race, ethnicity, age, ability or sexual orientation.
   - Listen to other people.
   - Be helpful to others.
   - Be patient.
   - Talk to someone in your class that you haven't talked to before.
   - Write a peace song.
   - Walk away from an argument.

   Adapted from www.benjerry.com/features/50_ways/50ways.cfm

   b Copy this line into your exercise book. For each suggestion for peace, decide where you would place it on the line.

   OF NO VALUE ——————————————————— A LOT OF VALUE

   c Explain to a partner why you have placed the suggestions at those points.

How can good relationships be developed between people?

A major way to create peace and harmony between people can be to ensure that there are good relationships between people.

Activities

3 Which of the words or terms in this list help to create good relationships between people? Try to give reasons for your answers.

> **Strong opinions**   **Different interests**   **Honesty**   **Trust**
> **Tolerance**   **Compromise**

Can you add any more words or terms of your own?

4 Look at the list of people below. Have you ever had 'conflict' or disagreements with any of these groups? What do you think caused the conflict?

> **Parents   Neighbours   Teachers   Friends at school   Brothers/sisters**

Must think about!

How many causes of conflict can you think of? Use the activities to help you. How many ways can peace be made and kept? (Don't forget 'talking about the problem'.)

What do the religions teach about peace?

All religious traditions have teachings about peace, whether it is 'inner peace' or peace between groups of people.

Christianity

During some church services, Christians are invited to 'share peace' with each other by shaking hands. Some Roman Catholic Christians would make a 'confession' to the priest, before taking Holy Communion if, for example, they had anger towards others.

Some Christians, such as Quakers, are 'pacifists' and will refuse to take part in war or conflict. They believe that peace should always be maintained. They may refer to the example of Jesus, who taught: 'Blessed are the peacemakers, for they will be called the children of God.' (*Matthew 5:9*)

Islam

Muslims often greet each other with messages of peace. In Arabic, *salaam* means 'peace' and a common greeting among Muslims is *Assalamu alaykum*, which means 'Peace be upon you'.

Buddhism

Buddhism encourages peace through the idea of *ahimsa* (not hurting or harming any living creature).

The Dalai Lama (the spiritual and political leader of Tibet) encouraged people to respond to violence with peace. For example, when China has used force in Tibet to put an end to opposition there, the Dalai Lama has called for a non-violent response. In fact, he won the Nobel Peace Prize in 1989.

Most religions would accept that the main way to achieve peace is through forgiveness and tolerance. You can read more about religious teachings on forgiveness on pages 24–27.

Can religion cause conflict?

Although religion has much to say on the subject of peace, it has been claimed that religion can actually be a cause of conflict. It has been pointed out that, throughout history, some of the most famous wars have been fought in the name of religion.

Activity

5 a In small groups of no more than four, try to think of at least two examples of when religion has caused conflict rather than peace. Share your ideas with the class.

b Why do you think religion might cause conflict rather than peace?

Research note

Find out about the reasons for:

The Crusades

The conflict in Northern Ireland

Did religion cause conflict or promote peace in these situations?

1.2 Peace (2)

The next two pages will help you to:

- analyse how communities work together for peace
- examine the role of interfaith dialogue in religion and conflict.

- **Do you agree with this quotation? Should religious believers be involved in politics?**

- **What has it got to do with them?**

'It isn't enough to talk about peace. One must believe in it. And it isn't enough to believe in it. One must work at it.'
Eleanor Roosevelt

How can communities work together?

How can peace be maintained and achieved?

There are many types of **conflict**. The most common are:

- global conflicts
- personal conflicts
- conflicts between communities.

Throughout the years, there have been several attempts to maintain peace, resulting in the formation of organisations and groups that work to achieve peace. Below are some examples.

Can religion help to make peace?

Religion cannot help on its own, but its leaders and worshippers can.

Must think about!

What should you do when your friends are arguing among themselves and you are stuck in the middle? How can you create peace between them?

Case study 1: The United Nations

The United Nations (UN) is an international organisation that works for global peace. Its stated aims are to make possible cooperation in:

- international law
- international security
- economic development
- social progress
- human rights
- achieving world peace.

It was founded in 1945 to stop wars between nations and to provide a platform for dialogue.

Case study 2: The Quakers

Who? The Religious Society of Friends (also known as the Quakers) has its roots in Christianity and is inspired by the Bible and the life and teachings of Jesus.

What? The Quakers teach the need for peace and equality. They are working to achieve positive social change in areas where there is a need for peace. Quakers are pacifists.

Where? They send peaceworkers to work in countries where there is unrest among communities. An example is Burundi, where peaceworkers have supported local groups who are trying to build stability in the country. They offer advice and support on how to maintain peace between communities.

How? In Britain, they are promoting the 'peace tax' campaign, calling for the government to use tax money for peace rather than war.

They offer courses aimed at adults working with children to teach them how to resolve issues of conflict.

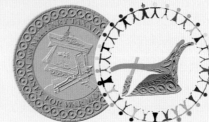

International Conference on War Tax Resistance and Peace Tax Campaign logo

How can different religions support peace by talking to each other?

A key concept here is **interfaith dialogue**, which is defined as exploring common ground between different faith groups.

Interfaith dialogue emphasises the need to work together and remove misunderstandings. Nevertheless, many people have different beliefs from those of their religious leaders and may choose not to take part in interfaith dialogue. Some religious believers do not see any need to understand different religious traditions. The Anglican Church is now actively trying to convert people of other faiths.

Some religious believers, particularly religious leaders, feel that taking part in interfaith dialogue is a good way of promoting peace and acceptance among differing religious traditions. It enables religious believers to have a greater understanding of different beliefs.

Activities

1 Look at the logo for the Quakers' 'peace tax' campaign on the opposite page. Design your own logo or advert for promoting peace.

2 Look at the following statements by two Heads of State. What do they tell you about the purpose of 'interfaith dialogue'?

   'If God wills it, we will then meet with our brothers from other religions, including those of the Torah and the Gospel… to come up with ways to safeguard humanity.'
   'The Saudi King calls for interfaith dialogue' (March 2008)

   'Different religions have different philosophical viewpoints but it is important to strengthen enthusiasm in their message of love, compassion and forgiveness which is common in all religion.'
   'The Dalai Lama talks with representatives of different religious faiths' (September, 2007)

Research note

Look at the case study about the Quakers. Can you create a similar case study for Neve Shalom/Wahat Al-Salam (Oasis of Peace)?

GradeStudio

Question

'Religion causes conflict not peace.' Do you agree? Give reasons or evidence for your answer, showing that you have thought of more than one point of view. You must include reference to religious beliefs in your answer.

(8 mark question, AO2)

This question tests your ability to evaluate differing points of view, including religious views (AO2). Levels will be used to measure the quality of your response. A good answer will explain, instead of simply describing, why religious believers may hold different views. Try to show how it links to other beliefs.

You could build an answer like this.

Level 1
First, express an opinion about the statement and give a reason or example to support it. For example, 'I don't agree. Most religions have teachings about peace and would try to promote peace whenever possible.'

Level 2
Next, expand your answer to include a religious teaching to support your opinion. For example, 'Christians encourage peace not conflict, because they follow the example of Jesus who preached that we should always forgive others.' Also offer a second example to support your opinion, for example 'Christians also say the Lord's Prayer, which tells them to forgive others.'

Level 3
Then, offer an alternative or different point of view and give a reason or example to support it. Try to include a religious teaching or moral reasoning to support the second view. For example, 'Other people might agree, because most of the wars throughout history have been fought in the name of religion. For example, during the Crusades, Christians and Muslims were told that they were fighting for God.'

Level 4
Finally, expand your answer to include a thorough discussion of the statement with several reasons/examples to support the differing viewpoints. Include several references to religious teachings related to the statement. For example, 'Buddhists would disagree with the statement, because their religion teaches *ahimsa*, which means non-violence to any living creature. This suggests that they should live peacefully, not in conflict. Other people might agree with the statement, because some religions do not promote interfaith dialogue. This suggests that they are not interested in keeping peace with other religions. This will eventually lead to conflict.'

1.3 Suffering (1)

The next two pages will help you to:

- examine the meaning and causes of suffering
- explore and evaluate the religious teachings on issues of suffering.

- Do you think that suffering can make someone a better person?

- Which do you feel is worse – to cause suffering or to ignore those who are suffering?

Must think about!

The cross has become a symbol of suffering and resurrection for those in the Christian faith. Try to design your own symbol for the relief of suffering in a troubled world.

Why do the innocent suffer?

People suffer in many different ways, for example through natural disasters, through ill health or because of other people's actions. To have to suffer through one's own fault may seem bad enough, but every day many suffer innocently and it is difficult to give a reason as to why this may be so. The world's religions have thought hard about this question for many generations.

What is suffering?

Suffering can be defined as 'patient endurance' – undergoing or bearing pain or distress. Some people have linked suffering to fate (a predetermined outcome); others to moral evil (caused by other humans) and to natural evil (earthquakes, floods).

Research note

Search newspapers and magazines for stories of suffering. Cut out photographs, headlines and paragraphs that you think best illustrate the troubles that people face. Choose also where help has been given and who gave it.

Create a collage of your findings and arrange them under a suitable heading, for instance 'A hurting world needs help'.

A Christian view

Some Christians argue that the world is 'corrupt' or 'fallen', and that there is an evil power in existence (Lucifer or Satan). Suffering comes as a result of original sin – a traditional doctrine that, because of the Fall of Man (*Genesis 2*), every human inherits a flawed nature in need of rebirth and with a tendency to sin.

There is also a view that, without suffering and evil, people would not really know what good is. Suffering and evil can reveal human weakness and help people to endeavour to put right the wrongs done.

Suffering is a result of God-given free will and it can assist individuals to grow spiritually or morally. It can be a test of faith (the story of Job) or a consequence of choosing right over wrong.

Nonetheless, Christians also believe that God is compassionate and understands the suffering of his people.

Christians are also exhorted to 'rejoice that you participate in the sufferings of Christ…'. (*1 Peter 4:13*)

A Muslim view

Muslims believe that humans are being tested through suffering in an impermanent world. Those who pass this test will find an eternal world that is perfect and infinite, while those who fail will see the evil consequences of their sins and corruption.

Most Muslims believe that, when they see a person who is sick, poor and needy, they are being tested by Allah for their charity and their faith. Good can come from suffering.

A Buddhist view

Buddhists teach why people suffer through the Four Noble Truths:

1 *Life means suffering*

This is because human nature is not perfect, nor is the world we live in. During their lifetime, people must endure physical suffering such as pain, sickness, injury, tiredness, old age and, eventually, death. They also must endure psychological suffering such as sadness, fear, frustration, disappointment and depression. Life is imperfect and incomplete, because our world is impermanent. Just as happy moments pass by, people and loved ones will pass away one day, too.

2 *The origin of suffering is attachment*

The origin of suffering is attachment to short-lived things, which include the physical world, and all objects of perception, as well as ideas. The reasons for suffering are craving and clinging. Because these objects of our attachment are short-lived, their loss is inevitable, and therefore suffering will follow.

3 *The end of suffering is possible*

The third Noble Truth expresses the idea that suffering can be ended by attaining 'dispassion'. This means that suffering can be overcome through human activity, simply by removing the cause of suffering. Attaining and perfecting dispassion is a process of many levels that ultimately results in the state of *nirvana*, which means freedom from all worries.

4 *The path to the cessation of suffering*

There is a path to the end of suffering – a gradual path of self-improvement, which is described in more detail in the Eightfold Path (see page 23).

Activities

1 Create a spider diagram showing the 'causes' of suffering. Try to include religious views in your answer as well as your own views.

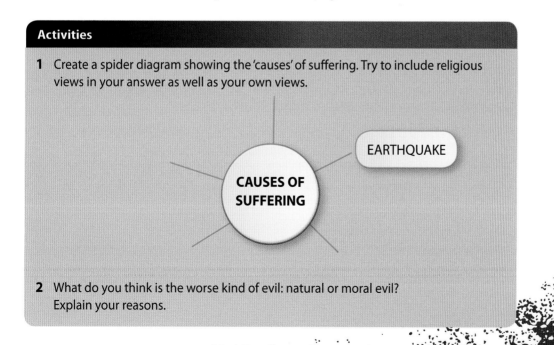

2 What do you think is the worse kind of evil: natural or moral evil? Explain your reasons.

1.4 Suffering (2)

The next two pages will help you to:

- debate what suffering means both to individuals and globally
- explore how those who are suffering can be helped through religious teachings and belief.

- If God is good, why does suffering happen?
- Is there a difference between a do-gooder and a charity worker?

CHARITY BEGINS AT HOME

Should we solve our own problems before we help others?

How can those suffering be helped?

There are many ways in which people's suffering can be eased. It all depends on the 'type' of suffering that the individual or group of people is enduring.

How do Christians respond to suffering?

Christians respond to suffering in various ways, including:

- through prayer – to relieve their own suffering or that of another person
- by reading the Bible
- by studying the lives of others who have suffered
- through a belief in an afterlife, where things will be better
- by believing that their suffering is part of a divine plan
- through service to others, possibly through charities working at home or abroad, or through working with the less fortunate.

Activities

1 a Draw the following chart in your exercise book and complete the second column. You can use the ideas suggested for help if you wish.

Type of suffering	How can they be helped?
Natural evil	
earthquake	
famine	
Moral evil	
breakdown of marriage due to affair	
loss of valuables due to burglary	

Ideas for help
Comfort from friends/
   relatives/counsellor
Acts of kindness
Charitable donations
Prayers
Aid work

   b What other types of suffering can you think of? Add your ideas to the chart and try to think of examples of ways in which suffering can be eased.

2 Research The Salvation Army and make a case study of its activities. Answer the questions, Who? What? Where? How? to organise your findings.

Sacred text

Then they also will answer, 'Lord, when was it that we saw you hungry or thirsty or a stranger or naked or sick or in prison, and did not take care of you?' Then he will answer them, 'Truly I tell you, just as you did not do it to one of the least of these, you did not do it to me.'

Matthew 25:44–45

How do Muslims respond to suffering?

- Through *zakat* – one of the Five Pillars. *Zakat* is the compulsory giving of 2.5 per cent of one's wealth each year to benefit the poor. It is regarded by Muslims as a type of worship and of self-purification. The Five Pillars are five duties that are compulsory to every Muslim. They are: *shahadah* (profession of faith), *salat* (prayer), *zakat* (giving to charity), *sawm* (fasting during *Ramadan)* and *hajj* (pilgrimage to *Makkah*).
- Through *sadaqah* (charity). This is a voluntary act of giving alms by Muslims who want to contribute more than their obligatory *zakat* payment. *Sadaqah* can be given during any period of happiness or sadness or as a sign of gratitude to Allah.
- Through accepting that whatever has happened is the will of Allah (*Insha' Allah*).
- Through the teachings of the Qur'an.

Sacred text

The Prophet (S.A.W.) said: 'Charity is a necessity for every Muslim.' He was then asked: 'What if a person has nothing?' The Prophet replied: 'He should work with his own hands for his benefit and then give something out of such earnings in charity.' The Companions asked: 'What if he is not able to work?' The Prophet said: 'He should help poor and needy persons'. The Companions further asked: 'What if he cannot do even that?' The Prophet said: 'He should urge others to do good.' The Companions said: 'What if he lacks that also?' The Prophet said: 'He should check himself from doing evil. That is also charity'.

Hadith

How do Buddhists respond to suffering?

Buddhists seek to understand and respond to suffering through the Eightfold Path:

1 **Right view** is the true understanding of the Four Noble Truths.
2 **Right aspiration** is the true desire to free oneself from attachment, ignorance and hatefulness.
3 **Right speech** involves abstaining from lying, gossiping or hurtful talk.
4 **Right action** involves abstaining from hurtful behaviour, such as killing and stealing.
5 **Right livelihood** means making your living in such a way as to avoid dishonesty and hurting others, including animals.
6 **Right effort** is a matter of exerting oneself with regard to the content of one's mind.
7 **Right mindfulness** is the focusing of one's attention on one's body, feelings, thoughts and consciousness in such a way as to overcome craving, hatred and ignorance.
8 **Right concentration** is meditating in such a way as to realise progressively a true understanding of imperfection, impermanence and non-separateness.

The Noble Eightfold Path

1.5 Forgiveness and reconciliation (1)

The next two pages will help you to:

■ examine the meaning of forgiveness from different viewpoints
■ explore religious teachings on the issue of forgiveness.

■ **Can you forgive your enemies?**

Men of the London Rifle Brigade meet the enemy in no man's land, Christmas Day, 1914

Is forgiveness possible?

Everyone has been involved in a conflict or arguments with someone they are close to. It can be very difficult to say sorry or to accept an apology in these situations. Imagine how much more difficult it would be if you had to forgive someone who had done you great harm or if you had to forgive an enemy!

Below are some possible scenarios in which people learned to forgive. For each example, consider whether *you* could have forgiven in that situation. Try to give a reason why or why not.

Family quick to forgive driver

Emily Jones' family has already forgiven the driver who killed her.

Police say that the driver momentarily lost concentration and crashed into the car, right where Emily was sitting.

The driver wasn't drunk or speeding. He may have been over-tired.

'I forgive them,' says mother

Two teenagers are found guilty of the unprovoked murder of Isaac Watson after a terrifying chase that led to his gruesome death.

How important is forgiveness?

Activity

1 Try to think of at least three reasons why you should forgive people who have treated you badly or caused you harm.

What are the religious teachings on forgiveness?

Christianity

Christianity teaches the example of Jesus, such as his teaching in the Beatitudes (*Matthew 5–7*), and the fact that he forgave his executioners when on the cross. In the Lord's Prayer, Christians ask God 'to forgive their sins, as they forgive those who have sinned against them'. There are also examples of Christians forgiving others, such as Martin Luther King, Jr.

Islam

Islam teaches that Allah will always forgive someone who is truly repentant, and that he will reward those who forgive others. All should pursue ways in which reconciliation can be achieved. Everyone should try and turn hatred into friendship by forgiveness and love. All descriptions of Allah show gentleness and tolerance. Allah provides safety and peace for all Muslims. There is the belief that Allah will always forgive someone who is penitent.

War should only be considered in the defence of Islam. There is the belief that Allah will always forgive someone who is truly penitent.

Buddhism

Buddhism teaches that forgiveness is a practice to prevent harmful thoughts from causing havoc to one's mental well-being. Buddhism recognises that feelings of hate have a lasting effect on our *karma*, and therefore encourages the cultivation of thoughts that have a wholesome effect.

Sacred texts

Love your enemies and pray for those who persecute you.
Matthew 5:44

For if you forgive others their trespasses, your heavenly Father will also forgive you.
Matthew 6:14

Sacred text

…those who control their anger and are forgiving towards people; Allah loves the good.
Qur'an 3:134

Sacred text

He abused me, he struck me, he overcame me, he robbed me – in those who harbour such thoughts hatred will never cease. He abused me, he struck me, he overcame me, he robbed me – in those who do not harbour such thoughts hatred will cease.
Dhammapada 1.3–4

Activities

2 Find and read the story of Zacchaeus (*Luke 19:1–9*).
   a What did Zacchaeus want to do?
   b What wrongs had Zacchaeus done?
   c How did Jesus show he forgave Zacchaeus?
   d What was Zacchaeus' response?
3 Write a short poem or song lyric on the theme of forgiveness.

Must think about!

What does it mean to 'forgive'?
- Make friends again?
- Forget the incident?
- Accept what has happened and move on?

Try to think of your own definition of 'forgiveness'.

If you forgive, does that mean that you should also forget?

1.6 Forgiveness and reconciliation (2)

- **Do people really deserve our forgiveness?**

Activities

1 **a** You have been asked to write an advert or an article for a magazine advertising Corrymeela (see p. 27). In your article, you will need to include: the situation that Corrymeela is trying to resolve, how they try to do this and WHY (religious teachings).

   b Visit the Corrymeela website to see pictures and extra information about their work.

2 Choose another religious tradition. Create a PowerPoint presentation or a leaflet about the work of Neve Shalom/Wahat al-Salam, or the Buddhist 'Holy Isle' project.

How important is it to forgive?

The concept of 'forgiveness' varies from person to person and in each situation. Sometimes people need to forgive a friend who has broken their trust, or a relative who has said something hurtful. In these situations, forgiveness is important in order to rebuild the relationship.

Occasionally, it may be necessary to forgive a person or a group of people who have caused harm but are complete strangers to you. An example of this is the Holocaust. Over six million people were murdered by the Nazis. Many surviving victims and relatives learned to forgive people that they did not know by name or face.

Why is this type of forgiveness necessary?

Most people would accept that forgiveness is important in order to move on from a painful event. Forgiveness is also important to create peace, particularly in situations of conflict and war.

A key word to remember here is **reconciliation** (bringing harmony to a situation of disagreement and discord).

How do people learn to forgive?

This is the hard part. Forgiveness does not come naturally to the majority of people. However, it is a teaching of most religious traditions. People may need help in order to forgive. This may involve mediation or counselling. Sometimes prayer can help, or studying sacred texts for guidance. On the next page is an example of a group that promotes forgiveness.

What can a religious agency do to build peace?

Corrymeela is a Christian peace-building centre and community on the north coast of Northern Ireland. It is often said that 'Corrymeela' means 'Hills of Harmony'. However, the name was already in existence when the centre at Ballycastle was bought by what became known as the 'Corrymeela Community'.

Its objective is to promote reconciliation and peace-building through the healing of social, religious and political divisions in Northern Ireland.

Corrymeela works with individuals and communities that have suffered through the violence of the conflict in Northern Ireland.

Their vision of Christian community and reconciliation has been expressed through 'a commitment to encounter, interaction and positive relationships between all kinds and conditions of people'.

Each year over 6,000 participants take part in programmes at Ballycastle, which has facilities for over 100 residents in three units.

Corrymeela's work can be categorised under five headings.

- School work on community relations issues, often through citizenship.
- Family work, providing respite and development work with groups.
- Faith and life, seeking to support individuals and church communities.
- Youth work, primarily focused on marginalised young people.
- Community work, looking at issues of intercommunity relations.

Corrymeela offers residential experience, which can create a new openness to deal with issues that people find difficult in the 'home' territory – often issues of reconciliation and community relations.

They believe that residential work needs to be related to work in the community. The residential work is frequently linked to community-based work. The experience supports change in people's ordinary day-to-day worlds, so that new patterns of activities and new structures are created, and institutions are influenced in positive directions.

 GradeStudio

Question

Explain from two religious traditions the work of an agency that promotes peace.

(6 mark question, AO1)

Levels will be used to measure the quality of your response. This question tests your ability to explain how and why religious organisations work for peace.

You could build an answer like this.

Level 1

First, make sure that you make a statement about the religious organisations and the situation they are trying to improve. For example, 'Corrymeela is a Christian agency trying to create peace in Northern Ireland between Catholics and Protestants. The Holy Isle project is a Buddhist community in Scotland trying to create peace between all faiths.'

Level 2

Then, give an example of how the agencies are working for peace. For example, 'Corrymeela organises residential courses to get people from different communities to talk to each other because Christians believe that this is one way to create peace. Holy Isle offers retreats for people of all faiths so that they can meet and talk to each other because Buddhists believe that interfaith dialogue is important.'

Level 3

Next, give more examples of the work that the agencies are doing to promote peace. For example, 'Corrymeela visits schools and provides workshops to encourage young people from different communities to communicate to work for peace. This is because educating the young is a vital part of their work. Holy Isle offers meditation sessions to help people to achieve inner peace. This is because meditation may be one way to help people develop.'

Level 4

Finally, draw together your ideas. Make sure that you have included several examples of how the agency is working for peace. Make sure that you have made good use of religious language. For example, 'Corrymeela believes that interfaith dialogue will encourage peace in Northern Ireland and prevent further conflict between religious communities. Corrymeela allows religious communities to benefit from the experiences of those who have visited Corrymeela and returned to Northern Ireland. Holy Isle believes that promoting spirituality through meditation and retreat can prevent conflict as people will get rid of anger. Buddhists believe that all people should live peaceful lives.'

1.7 Attitudes to conflict and war

The next two pages will help you to:

- express your own views on war, conflict and resolution
- begin to examine the concept of just war and religious teachings on this issue.

- Do you believe that you have the right to fight for what you believe is true?
- Would you choose violence as a first or last resort?

A JOIN TOGETHER TRAIN TOGETHER EMBARK TOGETHER FIGHT TOGETHER

LIEUT. JACKA V.C.

Enlist in the Sportsmen's Thousand

SHOW THE ENEMY WHAT AUSTRALIAN SPORTING MEN CAN DO.

B I WANT YOU TO DIE IN A FOREIGN DESERT FOR CORRUPT POLITICIANS

C BRITONS "WANTS" YOU JOIN YOUR COUNTRY'S ARMY! GOD SAVE THE KING

Activity

1. Above are three posters about war.

   a. Look at picture **A**. What impression of war does the poster give?

   b. Look at pictures **B** and **C**. What idea is each poster trying to convey?

   c. Which view do you most agree with? Try to give a reason.

Is it ever right to fight?

War and conflict are facts of life and have been around from the earliest periods in history. Sometimes it seems that the only way to resolve an argument is through conflict or war.

How can war/conflict be avoided?

A war should always be a last resort, once every other method of resolving the situation has been explored.

Activities

2. In pairs, discuss your own views on war. Is it acceptable to go to war? Are there other ways to resolve conflict?

3. Continuing in your pairs, think of a recent disagreement that you have been involved in. What was the cause? How was the situation resolved? With hindsight, was this the best way to resolve the situation?

4. Below is a list of ways in which conflict can be avoided. Put them in order starting with the method that you think would be the most successful.
   - Dialogue between leaders.
   - Impose sanctions on countries causing conflict (for example, refuse to trade with them).
   - Give in to the opposition's demands.
   - Send in the United Nations to negotiate.
   - Ignore the situation.
   - Send a message of peace and friendship.

In what ways do Buddhists choose to avoid fighting?

Buddhism, perhaps, has the best record of all religions for non-violence. Nothing in Buddhist scripture gives any support to the use of violence as a way to resolve conflict. The first precept of Buddhism is 'non-harming' (*ahimsa*): Buddhists reject violence and believe that compassion is the only answer to violence.

Buddhism is clearly pacifist in its teaching, and many Buddhists say quite bluntly that it is 'better to be killed than to kill'. Monks are allowed to defend themselves, but they must not kill, even in self defence.

But Buddhism, like the other great faiths, has not always lived up to its principles. There are numerous examples of Buddhists engaging in violence and even war. In the 14th century, Buddhist fighters led the uprising that evicted the Mongols from China. In Japan, Buddhist monks trained Samurai warriors in meditation that made them better fighters.

Buddhism makes a distinction between 'just' and 'unjust' wars. The use of force can be justified in certain circumstances. Participating in a just war need not be motivated by greed, hatred or delusion.

What does Islam think about fighting?

Jihad is taken to mean 'struggle'. The concept of jihad includes the idea of a struggling or striving to practise the Muslim faith effectively, or to defend it against enemies. When Muslims talk about a 'greater jihad' they refer to the inner spiritual struggle to live their lives for Allah. When they talk about a 'lesser jihad' they refer to the military struggle to defend Islam. Some of the rules for a 'lesser jihad' are:

- war should only be a last resort
- it should only be in defence
- it must be led by a spiritual leader
- trees, crops and animals should be protected
- the war should not continue when the enemy has surrendered
- civilians should not be harmed
- the aim of the war should be to restore peace and freedom
- there must be a reasonable chance of success
- to die fighting the jihad is to be assured of paradise as a martyr or witness
- enemies must first be offered the opportunity to convert to Islam. 'People of the Book' (Christians and Jews) can refuse to do this, but agree to Muslim rule, including payment of a special tax.

The Qur'an states that war should not be fought for reasons of greed or ambition to capture other lands. People should do what is pleasing to Allah, and that which fulfils humankind's role as a trustee (*khalifah*) on the earth.

Greater jihad, or conflict within oneself, is to work out what is right and what is wrong. Jihad can simply mean striving to live a moral and virtuous life, spreading and defending Islam, as well as fighting injustice. The Muslim's purest sacrifice is to struggle to live a perfect life and completely submit to Allah.

If a Muslim has experienced Allah and received guidance from the Qur'an, they struggle to apply that guidance in their everyday life. This is the spiritual struggle of the soul. In this instance, jihad is always there for the believer whether there is an external enemy or not.

The Christian view on just war follows on the next two pages.

Sacred texts

Hatred will not cease by hatred, but by love alone. This is the ancient law.

Dhammapada 1.5

Victory creates hatred. Defeat creates suffering. The wise ones desire neither victory nor defeat… Anger creates anger… He who kills will be killed. He who wins will be defeated… Revenge can only be overcome by abandoning revenge… The wise seek neither victory nor defeat.

Dhammapada 15.5

Sacred text

Fight in the cause of Allah those who fight with you, but do not go over the limits. Allah does not love the transgressors.

Surah 2:190

1.8 Just war

The next two pages will help you to:

- develop an understanding of just war and its principles
- debate the need for some religious believers to go to war.

- Look at this picture of St Thomas Aquinas. Does it suggest peace or war?

SAINT THOMAS AQUINAS
DOCTEUR DE L'EGLISE

Can a war ever be 'just'?

St Thomas Aquinas was born in 1225. He became a priest in 1250 and a Papal Adviser in 1259. He wrote the first conditions for **just war**, to which the Roman Catholic Church added others.

These are the conditions that must be satisfied for a war to be considered 'just'.

- **There must be a just cause.** This means that anyone being fought against must truly deserve it. War must not be an act of aggression, but a response to one.
- **The war must be started and controlled by the authority of state or ruler.** This means that only legitimate authority, such as the head of a government or country, can start a just war. It rules out civil war and rebellion.
- **The war must be for good, or against evil. Law and order must always be restored.** The war must not be due to greed, revenge or pride, but it could include protection, self-defence and prevention of a worse evil.
- **The war must be a last resort.** This means that every other option must be tried first.
- **There must be a reasonable chance of success.** This means that arms may not be used where there is no chance of winning.
- **The war must be fought proportionally.** This means that more force than is necessary should not be used or more civilians than necessary should not be killed.

How should a just war be fought?

- **Innocent people and non-combatants should not be harmed.** This includes not bombing civilian residential areas that include no military targets, and not committing acts of terrorism or reprisal.
- **Only appropriate force should be used.** This applies to both the sort of force and how much force is used.
- **Internationally agreed conventions regulating war must be obeyed.** Minimum force should be used. An attack or action must be intended to help in the military defeat of the enemy. It must be on a military objective, and the harm caused to civilians or civilian property must not be excessive in relation to the concrete and direct military advantage anticipated. This principle is meant to limit excessive and unnecessary death and destruction.

Activities

1 Research one war (for example, the Second World War, the First Gulf War). Using the just war principles, decide whether that war was a 'just' war.

2 Take a quick look at 'just war theory' on the Web or in an encyclopaedia. Can you identify the five principles that should be in place to end a just war?

Who are 'conscientious objectors'?

Conscientious objectors are people who, on religious, moral or ethical grounds, refuse to fight in a war or, in some cases, to take any role that would support any fighting forces.

Here are some of their arguments.

- Killing or harming another human being can never be justified.
- War is a waste of resources, and goes against the ideas of stewardship as given to humans by God.
- War causes too much suffering, especially of the innocent.
- War and armed fighting only stimulate the base and less desirable instincts in humans, such as prejudice, hatred, greed and selfishness.
- If a person is conscripted into the forces, this is a denial of their personal freedom, forcing them to go against their consciences, principles and beliefs.

Who are 'pacifists'?

Pacifism is when someone is opposed to war or violence as a means of settling disputes. A pacifist can be against war and violence because of their religious beliefs. For example, Quakers believe that violence and war go against the teachings of Christianity. They actively campaign for non-violence in the world. People who do not have religious beliefs may also be pacifists. They may feel that violence is morally wrong and will, therefore, refuse to take part in violence.

There have been many famous pacifists throughout history. Most were or are pacifists due to religious beliefs, for example:

- Martin Luther King, Jr
- Mohandas (Mahatma) Gandhi
- The Dalai Lama.

Arguments 'For'

- It is acceptable to take part in holy or just wars.
- While it is wrong to be involved in front-line fighting, it is acceptable to participate in other ways, such as hospital or medical support, chaplaincy or religious duties, personnel or counselling services.
- The greater good, in terms of the overall outcome, outweighs the evil and harm produced along the way.
- Self-defence is acceptable, as it is standing up for the defence of those unable to defend themselves.

Arguments 'Against'

- All kinds of war are contrary to religious teaching and, therefore, people should not get involved.
- War only succeeds in producing greater suffering and injustice, and encourages inappropriate or unhelpful attitudes that serve to divide people and nations.
- Participation in a war – in any way at all – is to be guilty of the violence and suffering war itself causes.
- Separating wars into different types of conflict does not change the moral and religious issues surrounding involvement in them.

> **For debate**
>
> Research and prepare for a class debate on the topic 'Religious believers are right to go to war.' Look carefully at the arguments for and against. The following ideas may help you.

1.9 Attitudes to non-violent protest

The next two pages will help you to:

- examine and evaluate the concept of non-violent protest
- study the viewpoint of non-violent protestors.

- Do you agree that there are valid ways to protest without using physical violence?
- Do you think that social change can be brought about through peaceful means?

How can non-violent protest be used?

Non-violent protest is the peaceful expression of disagreement. Examples of ways to demonstrate in this way include:

- writing letters of protest
- strikes
- peace sit-ins
- petitions
- banners
- hunger strikes
- wearing badges
- marches
- boycotts
- leaflets
- demonstrations.

Non-violent protest has been used to speak out on many issues, including:

- the environment
- human rights violations
- infringements against personal liberties.

Mohandas Gandhi, for example, led a long, non-violent struggle against British rule in India.

This powerful protest tool is often purely practical. Unlike pacifism, it is not necessarily built on spiritual or moral grounds. It can involve the use of:

- education
- persuasion
- civil disobedience
- non-cooperation.

What are some of the attitudes towards non-violent protest?

In the modern era, non-violent protest has been a frequent strategy used to try to bring about social change. However, it has not been popular with everyone and some philosophers and politicians have spoken against it. Many of its opponents believe that oppressed peoples should have the right to react violently in self-defence. Opponents also express the view that non-violent protest can impose the ideals and morals of one group on to another.

A useful way to look at non-violent protest is through the use of case studies.

Case study 1: Martin Luther King, Jr

- Martin Luther King, Jr (1929–1968) was a leader in the American Civil Rights Movement, which he had joined early in his life.
- He led the Montgomery Bus Boycott (1955–1956). This was organised after Rosa Parks, a black woman, refused to give up her seat on the bus to a white man – in the segregated south, black people could only sit at the back of the bus. The 382-day boycott led the bus company to change its regulations, and the Supreme Court declared such segregation unconstitutional.
- In 1957, he helped to found the Southern Christian Leadership Conference, formed to coordinate protests against discrimination. He advocated non-violent direct action based on the methods of Gandhi.
- In 1963, Martin Luther King, Jr led a famous march on Washington, where he delivered his 'I Have a Dream' speech, predicting a day when the promise of freedom and equality for all would become a reality in America.
- In 1964, he became the youngest person to receive the Nobel Peace Prize for his work to end segregation and racial discrimination through civil disobedience and other non-violent means.
- In 1965, he led a campaign to register blacks to vote. The same year the US Congress passed the Voting Rights Act, outlawing the practices of discrimination that had stopped blacks from voting in the south of the United States.
- On 4 April 1968, Martin Luther King, Jr was assassinated.

Activity

1 Research and write a short biography of Martin Luther King, Jr, describing his methods of peaceful protest and suggesting why he was so successful.

Case study 2: The Dalai Lama

- The Dalai Lama is a revered spiritual leader among Tibetans, but he describes himself as a simple Buddhist monk.
- He has been Head of the Tibetan Government in Exile in Dharamsala, India, since 1959.
- He has three commitments in life.
- His *first commitment* is the promotion of human values such as compassion, forgiveness, tolerance, contentment and self-discipline. He believes that all human beings are the same. Everyone wants happiness and does not want suffering. Even people who do not believe in religion recognise the importance of these human values in making their lives happier.
- His *second commitment* is the promotion of religious harmony and understanding among the world's major religious traditions. He believes that all major world religions have the same potential to create good human beings. All religious traditions must respect one another and recognise the value of each other's respective traditions. It is only as an individual that the doctrine of one religion, one truth, can be held.
- His *third commitment* concerns Tibet and its struggle for justice. This will cease to exist once a mutually beneficial solution is reached between the Tibetans and the Chinese.
- He is a man of peace. In 1989, he was awarded the Nobel Peace Prize for his non-violent struggle for the liberation of Tibet. He supports policies of non-violence, even in the face of extreme aggression.
- He was the first Nobel Laureate to be recognised for his concern for global environmental problems.
- Since 1959, he has received over 84 awards in recognition of his message of peace, non-violence and inter-religious understanding. He has also written over 70 books.

Activity

2 In your own words, explain how the Dalai Lama's commitments link to non-violent protest and can help bring peace in times of trouble.

1 Religion and conflict
Remember and Reflect

The questions in this section are based on the work you have done throughout this topic. Try to complete as many as you can.

The questions in set 1 are designed to test your factual recall and AO1 level skills (knowledge and understanding). The page numbers alongside the questions will help you to find information that might be useful for your answers. Use them to check against what you have written.

The questions in set 2 are more challenging, using AO2 level skills (use of evidence and reasoned argument to evaluate personal responses and differing viewpoints). Your answers may come from more than one part of the topic.

The suffering of Job

Set 1

1	Examine this picture. What does it tell you about Christian and Jewish ideas about suffering?	**pages 20–21**
2	Explain the meanings of the following key words:	**pages 14–15**

    a just war

    b reconciliation

    c pacifism

    d interfaith dialogue.

3 State two ways in which peace can be made. pages 16–17

4 Explain two causes of conflict. pages 16–17

5 Describe two religious teachings about peace. pages 16–17

6 Describe two examples of interfaith dialogue. pages 18–19

7 Explain two religious teachings about suffering. pages 20–21

8 Choose two agencies that work for peace. Describe one similarity and one difference between the two. pages 18–19

9 State an example of natural evil and an example of moral evil. pages 22–23

10 Give three examples of how suffering can be overcome. pages 22–23

11 Which religious traditions may say that sometimes war is acceptable? pages 28–31

12 Which religious traditions are against war under any circumstances? pages 28–31

13 Choose one individual who has used non-violent protest. Describe three key points about his or her life and work. pages 32–33

Set 2

14 Answer the following questions, giving as much detail in your answers as possible:

  a Do you think that it is important to maintain peace? Give reasons for your answer.

  b Do you think that non-violent protest is a good way to get what you want?
  Try to consider more than one point of view.

  c Can we ever fully forgive our enemies? Give reasons for your answer.

15 *'Religious believers should spend more time worshipping God and less time worrying about suffering in the world.'*

Choose two religious traditions and try to explain what their response to this statement would be. Remember that there may be different opinions within religious traditions.

16 *'Religious believers should be conscientious objectors.'*

Choose two religious traditions and try to explain what their response to this statement would be. Remember that there may be different opinions within religious traditions.

17 As a class, debate the following statement:

'There can't be such a thing as God. If there was, he would stop our suffering.'

On these pages you will find the types of question you might encounter in the exam, along with sample answers and comments. A good understanding of this information may help you to improve the content and structure of your own answers.

You may wish to refer to the level descriptor grids in the Introduction (pages 10–11).

Question

Explain how having religious faith might help someone who is suffering. (4 mark question, AO1)

Level 1	Level 2
First, make a simple link between what religious believers think and what they do. For example, 'Having religious faith might help someone who is suffering because they can pray to God.'	Next, make a clear link between the teachings on suffering and what a believer might do. For example, 'Christians believe that praying can help because God may end their suffering or may provide them with an answer.'
Level 3	**Level 4**
Then, describe another reason why having religious faith might help someone who is suffering. Try to bring in religious language. For example, 'Having faith would help someone who is suffering, because they may turn to scriptures for help.'	Finally, make sure that you have described in detail the teachings that help believers when suffering. Try to make good use of religious terms and interpret them correctly. For example, 'Christians and Jews may turn to the book of Job, which shows Job suffering because God was allowing him to be tested.'

Question

'Using violence is always wrong.' Do you agree? Give reasons or evidence for your answer, showing that you have thought of more than one point of view. You must include reference to religious beliefs in your answer. (8 mark question, AO2)

This question tests students' ability to evaluate different ideas about non-violence and to provide evidence for these ideas. Levels will be used to measure the quality of your response. A good answer will not only describe a point of view, but will also explain it in detail, and show some awareness of how it links to other religious beliefs and affects the life of a believer. A good answer should also recognise that there may be alternative viewpoints about the issue.

Student's answer

I agree because most religious traditions teach that it is wrong to use violence because we should work for peace. (Level 1) An example of this is Christianity and the teachings of Jesus.

Other people may disagree because they think that violence is the only way to solve things. Peaceful protests don't work because people take no notice. (Level 2)

Comments

The student gave a clear opinion along with a reason for this view, which included reference to religious teachings. This puts the answer at Level 1. The student then went on to give another point of view with a justification for that view, which earned Level 2.

To reach Level 3, the student would have to explain both points of view in more detail, referring to religious or moral ideas about the statement. To reach Level 4, they would need to discuss thoroughly the idea of 'non-violence', perhaps by giving examples of people who have campaigned non-violently and their reasons for these beliefs. They should also consider different religious views about non-violence, perhaps mentioning the idea of just war.

Student's improved answer

I agree, because most religious traditions teach that it is wrong to use violence because we should work for peace. An example of this is Christianity and the teachings of Jesus. **(Level 1)** Jesus taught that violence is wrong. An example of this is when he told his friends to put down their swords because 'Those who live by the sword will die by the sword.' **(Level 2)** Christians like Martin Luther King, Jr have followed Jesus' example and used non-violence in their campaigns.

Other religious traditions such as Buddhism also have teachings on non-violence. The idea of 'ahimsa' means non-violence to all living creatures, so a Buddhist may agree with the statement. **(Level 3)**

Other people may disagree because they think that violence is the only way to solve things. Peaceful protests don't work because people take no notice. Some religious believers may say that it is ok to use violence in some circumstances. This is because their religious traditions may have guidelines about going to war. In Christianity, these are called the just war principles. These may mean that non-violence isn't always the answer. **(Level 4)**

Question

'All suffering comes from God.' Give two reasons why a religious believer might agree or disagree with this statement.

(4 mark question, AO2)

Level 1 A simple appropriate justification of a point of view.	First, show you understand the question and state an opinion. For example, a religious believer may disagree because God is supposed to be good so he wouldn't let us suffer.
Level 2 An expanded justification of one point of view, which includes religious teaching OR two simple points of view.	Next, justify this view by referring to religious teachings. For example, in Christianity, the Bible states that Adam and Eve used their free will to disobey God. This means that the world is no longer perfect so this is why we suffer.
Level 3 An expanded justification of one point of view, with appropriate example and/or illustration, which includes religious teaching. In addition, a second simple appropriate justification of a point of view.	Then, offer a deeper explanation of the first point and add a second opinion about the statement. For example, this means that all humans are born with evil in them called 'original sin', which causes us to do wrong and make others suffer. A religious believer might also disagree with the statement because they think the Devil causes suffering.
Level 4 An expanded justification of two viewpoints, incorporating the religious teaching and moral aspects at issue and their implications for the individual and the rest of society.	Some Christians believe that the Devil is a fallen angel who works against God to cause suffering. Therefore suffering does not come from God.

2 Religion and medicine

The Big Picture

- In this topic you will be addressing various medical ethics relating to religion and medicine.
- This topic covers three principal religions: Christianity, Judaism and Sikhism.
- You will need to focus on at least two principal religions.

You will look at:

- religious teachings about the sanctity of life
- the role that conscience plays in making life and death choices
- some ways that are used to support people making difficult medical decisions
- religious practices and teachings about abortion
- rights and choices concerning abortion
- rights and choices concerning euthanasia
- ethical issues surrounding in vitro fertilisation (IVF).

You will also think about the different attitudes that exist towards these ethics and practices.

What?

You will:

- develop your knowledge and understanding of medical ethical terminology
- develop your knowledge and understanding of religious teaching on the issues of sanctity of life, abortion, euthanasia and IVF
- gain an understanding of the Hippocratic Oath and the dilemmas of considering life and death decisions
- make links with the subjects and your own beliefs.

Why?

Because:

- these are major areas of discussion in today's world and in the media
- there are different sides to how people view these subjects
- it is impossible to live in 21st-century Britain and not know someone who has faced at least one of these dilemmas.

How?

By:

- learning and recalling the teaching of two world faiths on these issues
- thinking about the relevance of these teachings in the world today
- referring to different cases and examples that illustrate these issues
- analysing others' points of view and comparing them to your own.

Quiz

1   How many attempts at IVF are there in Britain each year?
    a) 4000   **b)** 15,000   **c)** 45,000

2   How many states in the USA allow euthanasia?
    a) 2   **b)** 10   **c)** 19

3   Which of the following is not a method of fertility treatment?
    a) IVF   **b)** AID   **c)** CID

4   Which of the following can be transplanted?
    a) eyes   **b)** face   **c)** heart   **d)** brain

5   When does a foetus's heart begin to beat?
    a) 1–2 weeks   **b)** 5–6 weeks   **c)** 14–16 weeks

6   In how many countries is abortion illegal?
    a) 5   **b)** 10   **c)** 32   **d)** 52

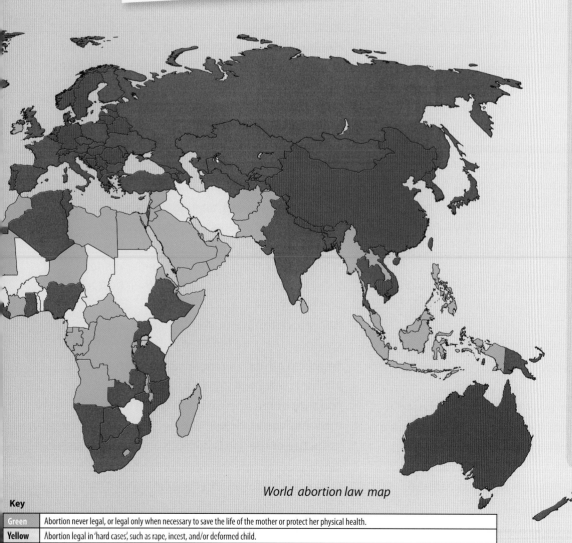

World abortion law map

Key	
Green	Abortion never legal, or legal only when necessary to save the life of the mother or protect her physical health.
Yellow	Abortion legal in 'hard cases', such as rape, incest, and/or deformed child.
Red	Abortion legal for social reasons (e.g. mother says she can't afford a child), or to protect the mother's 'mental health' (definitions and requirements vary).
Purple	Abortion legal at any time during pregnancy for any reason.

Adapted from www.pregnantpause.org/lex/world02map.htm

Activities

1   Individually, complete the quiz. Check your answers against the correct answers at the bottom of the page.

    1–2 correct. You have little knowledge about medical issues at the moment. You will know more by the end of this topic.

    3–4 correct. You have some knowledge about medical issues, but you will know more by the end of the topic.

    5–6 correct. You have good knowledge about medical ethics. Use this topic to further develop your knowledge.

2   Do any of the answers surprise you? If so, which ones and why? Explain your thoughts to a partner or to the class.

Answers
1c; 2a; 3c; 4c; 5b; 6d

Develop Your Knowledge

This topic is about religion and medicine. Read the information below, which will help you to think about the issues before you begin more detailed work.

Key information

- Most religious traditions (with the exception of Buddhism) believe that humans are created in the image of God and that, therefore, life is special.

- With advances in scientific technology, it has become possible to control life and death in a way that people could never have imagined only a few decades ago.

- There are many issues relating to medical ethics. Often people are required to make decisions regarding life and death situations. These decisions can be very difficult, as they may affect a number of people, not just themselves.

- Some medical advances were not around when religious texts were written, so there may be no specific guidance on medical ethics in religious texts. In these situations, making a decision concerning life and death can be tricky.

- When making ethical decisions, doctors must remember that they have made a promise, such as that in the 'Hippocratic Oath'.

- Religious guidelines, free will and conscience all have a part to play when making decisions about ethical dilemmas.

- Abortion raises issues about the rights of the unborn child.

- Whether to have an abortion is a difficult decision for anyone to make.

- The end of life is an important time for both the person who is dying and their family and friends. It is debatable who has the right to say when death should come.

- Drug therapy, hospitalisation, psychiatric treatment, physiotherapy and palliative care are all considered alternatives to euthanasia when someone is extremely unwell.

- There is a range of views for and against IVF.

Key words

abortion ending a pregnancy by removing an embryo or foetus from the womb; this results in the death of the embryo or foetus

blood transfusion the transfer of blood to another person

cloning the process of making an identical copy of something (the problem being that any defects, illnesses, etc. are also copied)

conscience an innate moral sense that guides actions and responses

euthanasia literally means 'good death'; it means helping someone to die in a painless manner

*free will the belief that nothing is determined

genetic engineering altering the structure and characteristic of a gene; this is done for many reasons, such as to improve the quality of crops and foods

*Hippocratic Oath a special promise made by those working in medicine to do their best to preserve a life

IVF stands for 'in vitro fertilisation', and is when a sperm and egg are fertilised outside the womb

*medical ethics the moral principles that affect medical issues and practice

*quality of life the extent to which life is meaningful and pleasurable

*sanctity of life life is precious and utterly priceless

surrogacy an arrangement where one woman carries a child for another couple

*We draw attention to these key words in particular because they are the ones that appear in the WJEC specification.

Key questions

- Why is life so special?
- Should people have free will to make life/death decisions?
- What are the moral issues a couple must consider in life and death decisions?
- How do doctors make ethical decisions?
- What are the dilemmas faced by scientific advancements?
- How can a religion help or hinder people making decisions?
- Does the decision depend on the situation?
- What are the rights of the unborn child?
- Whose choice should it be concerning the issue of abortion?
- Whose life is it anyway?
- Is it ever right to end someone's life?
- Is it right to spend so much money on IVF when people are starving in the world?

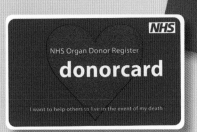

For interest.

Did you know?

- Nearly 400 people die every year in the UK while waiting for a transplant. More than 5,500 people in the UK are waiting for an organ transplant. They must wait for a suitable donor.
  NHS Direct

- The government is considering changing the law so that everyone is automatically on the organ donors' list, unless they request not to be.

Important questions

- Should everyone be made to be an organ donor?
- Should parents who lose a child be forced to donate the child's organs?

2.1 Sanctity of life (1)

The next two pages will help you to:

- examine and develop your own viewpoints on why life is special
- begin to explore issues of life and death, and how tough decisions relating to them sometimes have to be made.

- **What is more important, the quality of life or the sanctity of life?**

Why is life so special?

Most religious traditions (with the exception of Buddhism) believe that humans are created in the image of God and that, therefore, life is special. Because of this, they believe that none of us asked to be born, and that human life is precious. It deserves special respect and treatment. Some also believe that God has a plan for every human life and that each person matters. Therefore, life should never be taken intentionally.

Activity

1 a Read the *Sacred texts*. In pairs, discuss what you think is the meaning of each quotation. How do they show that life is special?

b Think of three reasons of your own to explain why life is special.

Sacred texts

In his hand is the life of every living thing and the breath of every human being.
Job 12:10

You created every part of me; you put me together in my mother's womb.
Psalm 139:13

You know everything I do, from far away you understand all my thoughts.
Psalm 139:2

God sends us and we take birth. God calls us back and we die.
Adi Granth 1239

Should people have free will to make life/death decisions?

Some key words to remember here are **sanctity of life** (that life is precious and utterly priceless) and **quality of life** (the extent to which life is meaningful and pleasurable).

With the advances in scientific technology, it has become possible to control life and death in a way that people could never have imagined only a few decades ago. Many people feel that it is our right to use technology in order to create, preserve or even end life. However, this issue can often cause debate among religious believers.

On the next page are some arguments concerning this debate.

2 a Look at the table below. Individually, decide which statements suggest that we should have the free will to make life and death decisions.

  b Now decide which statements suggest that we do not have the right to make life and death decisions.

  c Try to think of at least one more argument for each column.

  d Which arguments would be supported by religious believers?

	For	Against
All humans are sacred and special so they should be allowed to die with dignity		
Life is a gift, so we should try to preserve it.		
All human life is special, so we don't have the right to interfere with it.		
God gives life, so only he can take it away.		
It is my life, so I should be able to make my own decisions.		

What about religious teachings on the sanctity of life?

I am a Sikh. I believe that all life is precious, because human life is created by Waheguru and Waheguru is in all living things. My holy book, the Guru Granth Sahib, states: 'God is the destroyer, preserver and creator'. (Japji Sahib 5) This means that God is in control of life.

I am a Jew. Our holy book – the Torah – says that all life is holy and sacred, because it is created by God. Humans were created in God's image and are therefore important. The Torah says, 'So God created man in his own image.' (Genesis 1)

I am a Christian. I believe that all life should be valued, because we are all part of God's creation. Only God can create life and only he can take it away. Jesus' miracles and parables also show that human life should be valued and preserved.

2.2 Sanctity of life (2)

The next two pages will help you to:

- examine your own response to a range of moral issues related to life and death – such as organ donation
- evaluate religious responses to these issues.

- **Should we donate organs when we die?**

What are the moral issues a couple must consider in life and death decisions?

There are many issues relating to **medical ethics**. People are often required to make decisions regarding life and death situations. These decisions can be very difficult, as they may affect a number of people, not just themselves. The following questions or dilemmas frequently appear when making decisions concerning life and death.

- Is it right to take organs from a person to use for donation once that person has died?
- Should we have their permission?
- What if that would mean saving a life?
- Should we break the law if it means obeying the wish of a loved one (for example, euthanasia)?
- Should we follow the teachings of our religious tradition even if we don't fully agree with the teachings?
- Should we just accept our situation and not try to change it?

Can religion help?

Sometimes having religious beliefs can help when making life and death decisions. Religious traditions often have clear teachings about medical ethics, which you will be able to explore in the following pages. Religious believers can turn to their sacred texts for guidance or ask a religious leader for advice.

However, some medical advances were not around when religious texts were written, so there may be no specific guidance on medical ethics in religious texts. In these situations, making a decision concerning life and death can be difficult.

Activity

1 In pairs, choose two of the dilemmas and discuss your thoughts on them. Record your thoughts in the form of a PMI chart, like the one shown below.

	Plus	Minus	Interesting
Arguments in support			
Arguments against			

Sometimes religious believers are required to look at general teachings concerning life and death and try to apply them to their own situation. It may be helpful for them to:

- search sacred texts
- speak to a religious leader
- pray
- weigh up pros and cons.

Occasionally, a religious believer may not agree with the teachings of their religious tradition, and must decide then whether or not to follow those teachings. They may believe in **free will**, and choose to follow their own **conscience**.

Activities

2 a In groups of no more than four, make a list of all of the body parts that you know can be donated.

   b Can any of these be transplanted while a person is still alive?

3 a Look at these different viewpoints:

   'I am a Protestant Christian. I have been taught that it is good to donate organs as it is an act of charity.'

   'I am a Jehovah's Witness. Organ donation isn't really promoted in my tradition.'

   'I am a Jehovah's Witness. People in my religious tradition have refused blood transfusions.'

   'I am a Roman Catholic. I think that it is good to donate organs, because it helps others to live. Life is precious, as it is a gift from God.'

   'I am a Jew. My religious tradition teaches that organ donation is good, as it saves lives.'

   'I am an Orthodox Jew. We are not allowed to donate organs, unless there is a recipient waiting for the organ. We can't just donate them to an organ bank.'

   'I am a Jew. I think that it is difficult to decide whether to donate organs, particularly hearts. If the heart is still beating, that person is still alive according to Jewish Law, so we would be killing that person.'

   b Ask yourself: Why might a Christian find it difficult to make a decision about organ donation? What dilemmas might a Jew face concerning organ donation?

Must think about!

Consider the following questions:

- Are transplants a waste of money?
- If a person abuses their body, for example with cigarettes, drugs or alcohol, should they be allowed a transplant?
- Should doctors play God and extend people's lives?

Definition – organ donation

Organ transplants are when an organ, for example the heart or kidney, is taken from one person's body and placed in someone else's. It is also now possible to use organs grown on animals. A dilemma that a religious believer might face could be about organ donation. As there are various views within each religious tradition, this could cause a problem for religious believers.

GradeStudio

Question

'The "quality of life" is more important than the "sanctity of life".' Give two reasons why a religious believer might agree or disagree with this statement. *(4 mark question, AO2)*

This question tests your ability to explain a religious point of view (AO2). Levels will be used to measure the quality of your response. A good answer will explain instead of simply describing why religious believers may hold different views. Try to show how it links to other beliefs.

You could build an answer like this.

Level 1

First, show that you understand the question and state an opinion. For example, 'A religious believer might disagree, because there are teachings about the sanctity of life in all religious traditions.'

Level 2

Next, justify this view by referring to religious teachings. For example, 'In Judaism, it states that life is precious and belongs to God.'

Level 3

Then, offer a deeper explanation of the first point and add a second opinion about the statement. For example, 'This suggests that we don't have the right to end life, if we don't have a good quality of life. A Jew would agree because they also see life as being very important.'

Level 4

Finally, develop the second viewpoint to include a religious teaching to support the viewpoint. For example, 'Jews teach that it is important to put aside laws to save life. This implies that being alive is more important than if the person has quality of life.'

2.3 Medical ethics (1)

The next two pages will help you to:

- explore sensitive ethical issues such as genetic engineering
- examine religious responses and teachings related to these issues.

How do doctors make ethical decisions?

Medical ethics concern the right and wrong way people should behave in medical matters. When making ethical decisions, doctors must remember that they have made a promise, such as that in the **Hippocratic Oath**.

What is the Hippocratic Oath?

This is a special promise that has been made by those working in medicine to do their best to preserve life. Although the original Hippocratic Oath is rarely used nowadays, all doctors take an oath to uphold the standards of their profession and also to conduct themselves in a professional manner.

Nurses also have a code of conduct, which states that they must:

- respect the patient or client as an individual
- obtain consent before giving any treatment or care
- cooperate with others in the team
- protect confidential information
- maintain their professional knowledge and competence
- be trustworthy
- act to identify and minimise the risk to patients and clients.

What are the dilemmas faced by scientific advancements?

Besides abortion, euthanasia and IVF, recent scientific advances include cloning, organ transplants, blood transfusions and genetic engineering. Scientific advances mean that humans are often required to make life and death decisions that didn't exist in the past.

There are often dilemmas surrounding these cases. This is particularly so for religious believers. Some feel that such advances are good, because they allow us to create and preserve life that is 'sacred'. Others feel uncomfortable with the idea of 'playing God'. What about surrogacy as a moral dilemma?

What are some typical medical dilemmas?

Read the following case studies and answer the questions for each.

Case study 1

A 30-year-old mother died shortly after giving birth to her first son. The mother had lost a lot of blood during the birth. The woman could have been saved with a simple blood transfusion, but she had signed a declaration forbidding doctors to give her a transfusion.

- Why do you think the woman in the story refused a blood transfusion?

Case study 2

A British couple, who were trying for a baby, discovered that they were both carriers of a genetic defect known as cystic fibrosis. They were able to use genetic screening to see whether the baby would have cystic fibrosis or not. At the moment, if the baby were to have cystic fibrosis, their only options would be to progress with the pregnancy or to have a termination. Most people affected by cystic fibrosis live until adulthood.

In the future, there may be an option to use genetic engineering to alter the gene within the embryo that carries cystic fibrosis.

- Is it acceptable to alter the genes of a foetus in order to eradicate defects? Try to give reasons for and against.
- What do you think a religious believer would say about this?

Christian teaching on genetic engineering

Views against:

- If God wanted the results of genetic engineering to happen, then he would have created them as such.
- Man has no right to play God.
- It can be seen as immoral and unnatural, as it interferes with nature.

View for:

- If God has given us talents, we should use them.

Judaism teaching on genetic engineering

- It is prohibited in Jewish Law to marry a woman from a family of epileptics or lepers in case the illness is transmitted to future generations.

Sikhism teaching on genetic engineering

- Genetic engineering to cure a disease is acceptable.
- Human cloning is not acceptable.

Activity

1 'Think, pair, share' the following questions and statements – *Think about it, discuss with a partner, share with the class*:

   a Is it right to screen for incurable genetic diseases that do not show themselves till middle age, such as Huntingdon's disease?

   b Screening will prevent the disease being passed on, but it will also destroy the life of the person who hasn't yet shown symptoms of the disease, by filling even their pre-symptomatic period with fear.

   c What about someone found to be a carrier of a genetic disease:
   - should they get married?
   - should they disclose their carrier status to a possible partner – and at what stage in the relationship?
   - should they ask about the carrier status of a prospective partner – and at what stage in the relationship?
   - should mass population screening be carried out for such diseases?

Definition – genetic engineering

Genetic engineering uses the techniques of molecular cloning and transformation to alter the structure and characteristics of genes. In the past, humans have brought about change in the genetic make-up of organisms by means of selective breeding. Genetic engineering brings about such change by scientifically altering an organism's genetic code.

Sikhs believe that human life begins at conception. There is a view among many Sikhs that altering the genetic makeup of a foetus is interfering with nature. Sikhs have great respect for the natural form and believe it should not be tampered with. If a couple knows that there is a risk of passing on a genetic disorder they should use contraceptive means to avoid it. Some consultants, however, think that this scientific knowledge is God given and should be used to benefit humanity.

Owen Cole, 2005

2.4 Medical ethics (2)

The next two pages will help you to:

- analyse the concept of medical ethics and explore ethical dilemmas
- examine the religious teachings related to these issues and whether they clarify outcomes.

- **What has religion got to do with medical ethics?**
- **Why do you think people are concerned about the idea of 'cloning'?**

Dolly the sheep was the first mammal to be cloned from the DNA of an adult mammal

How does a religion help or hinder people making decisions?

The question of whether religion helps or hinders people in making ethical and medical decisions is highly debatable.

Activity

1 As a class, make a list or spider diagram of all the areas that may be covered under the topic of 'medical ethics'. One example might be abortion.

Medical ethics

Do the different religions agree?

Christianity

There is no single official view and Christians may even differ in their response to their own denomination's viewpoint. In the conflict between faith and science, few church leaders go as far as spelling out which medical procedures are right and which are wrong.

Roman Catholicism and some other Christian denominations believe that the soul enters the body at the moment of conception (when the sperm and egg unite). They believe harvesting cells for embryonic cloning is the same as live human experimentation and is contrary to God's will.

In 2000, the Pope endorsed voluntary organ donation for Catholics, calling it *'a genuine act of love'*.

Jehovah's Witnesses believe that, since life is a gift from God, blood should not be intermingled. Provided the donated organ is clear of the donor's blood, it is possible for organ transplants to take place.

Judaism

If a blood transfusion is deemed medically necessary, then it is not only permissible, but obligatory in Judaism. There is no law against blood transfusions. On the contrary, life is deemed the most important thing in the Hebrew scriptures. One must do everything within one's power (except idolatry, unlawful sexual unions or murder) to save a human life.

Whether it is loss of life or serious illness, many Jews see only receiving blood as an alternative: 'Blood is life.'

Sikhism

Sikhs derive their ethics largely from the teachings after their scripture, the Guru Granth Sahib, and the Sikh Code of Conduct (the Rehat Maryada).

Guidance also comes from the example set by the gurus, and from the experience of the Sikh community over the last 500 years. These do not give detailed ethical answers, but set down general principles and provide a framework to help Sikhs answer such questions.

Sikhs believe in life after death, and a continuous cycle of rebirth. However, they do not need the physical body in this cycle. The soul of a person is eternal, but the body is simply flesh and is perishable.

Does the decision depend on the situation?

The majority of religious believers feel very strongly about their faith and would seek to follow their religious teachings about medical matters. However, they may feel differently if put in a real life situation concerning medical ethics. In some religious traditions, particularly Christianity, there is a variety of teachings which may be open to interpretation.

In addition to religious guidelines, free will and conscience both have a role to play when facing ethical dilemmas.

For debate

Research and prepare for two class debates on:

- We should make up our own minds about medical ethics.
- We must always follow the laws of our religion or country when making ethical decisions.

Debate each point of view.

Activities

2 Create a Venn diagram showing the similarities and differences in the teachings of Christianity and two other religious traditions concerning medical ethics (including organ donation and genetic engineering).

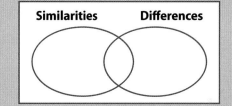

3 a Read the statements from the following religious believers.

b Both characters are Christians. How are their views on making ethical decisions different?

2.5 Abortion (1)

The next two pages will help you to:

- explore the sensitive topic of abortion and examine your own views relating to it
- analyse, through religious teachings, the rights of the unborn child.

- Who owns your body?
- When does life begin?

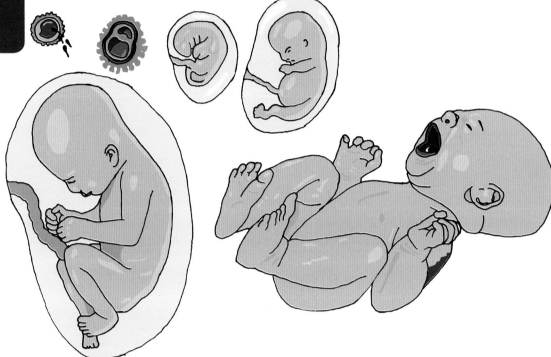

The development of a foetus

What are the rights of the unborn child?

An answer to this question must include consideration of both the sanctity of life and the quality of life of both an embryo and the mother. It prompts other questions: Does abortion deny the rights of the unborn child? And in what circumstances is abortion felt to be permissible?

What is an abortion?

An abortion is the removal of an embryo or foetus from the uterus, resulting in its death.

What are the grounds for an abortion in Britain?

An abortion can take place up to 24 weeks into the pregnancy.

Two doctors must decide that there will be a risk to a woman's physical or mental health or a risk to her already existing child(ren)'s physical or mental health if she goes ahead with the pregnancy.

Abortions can be performed after 24 weeks in extreme circumstances, such as evidence of severe foetal abnormality or grave risk to the life of the woman.

For interest

Some startling facts

- In Britain – which has one of the highest rates of teenage pregnancies in Western Europe – 4,376 abortions were performed on girls aged under 16 in 2007 (up 10 per cent). There were also 163 on girls under 14 (up 21 per cent).
- The youngest mother in Britain was aged 12 years and 8 months.
- The youngest mother in the world was 5 years old.

What do religions teach on the rights of the unborn child?

Christian teaching

Christians are concerned with the rights of the unborn child, because of their belief:

- in the sanctity of life
- in the preciousness of life
- that humans are made in the image of God.

There is no single Christian view on abortion. Some Christians may not even agree with their own denomination's official point of view.

Roman Catholic and Orthodox Churches

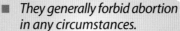

- *They generally forbid abortion in any circumstances.*
- *They believe that life begins at conception.*
- *They believe that life is sacred.*

- *Many support the 'pro-life' opinion that life is precious and must be preserved.*
- *Some may allow abortion in specific circumstances such as rape.*

Evangelical Protestants

- Other denominations tend to be against abortion carried out for social reasons (for example, a lifestyle choice), but accept that, in some circumstances, it may be a preferred choice (such as when to decide between the life of the mother or the child).

- Many Christian denominations allow the individual to make up their own mind whether abortion is right or wrong in those particular circumstances.

Judaism teaching

Judaism does not allow anyone purposefully to cause a woman to miscarry. The rights of the unborn child are of the greatest importance.

Orthodox Jews

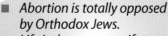

- *Abortion is totally opposed by Orthodox Jews.*
- *Life is the greatest gift to mankind and must be preserved.*
- *The Creator alone can take life.*

- *Abortion is permitted in some circumstances, such as when the mother's life is at risk.*
- *Each case is unique and must be treated as such.*
- *Some Jews allow abortion if the pregnancy was a result of rape or incest.*

Progressive Jews

Sikhism teaching

- Sikhs believe that life begins at the moment of conception. It is a sin to destroy life, so deliberate miscarriage or abortion is forbidden.
- However, the Rehat Maryada (Sikh Code of Conduct) does not mention abortion, so there are some circumstances in which some Sikhs allow abortion:
  - If the child is likely to be born with deformities.
  - If the woman has become pregnant as a result of rape.
  - If the woman's life is in danger due to ill health during pregnancy.

Despite these teachings, there is a concern that, in India, the practice of aborting female embryos due to a preference for sons is growing.

Activities

1 Answer these questions from your point of view.
- Does the age of the woman make any difference concerning rights for abortion?
- If a girl becomes pregnant, who has the right to decide on an abortion?
- Who should have the right? Why?
- What if one parent wants an abortion and the other doesn't?
- How many abortions should a woman be allowed to have?
- Should abortions be free on the National Health Service (NHS)?

2 Create a poster for a religious tradition of your choice. Your poster should argue the point of view of your religious tradition concerning abortion. You should include religious teachings in your poster.

2.6 Abortion (2)

The next two pages will help you to:

- consolidate your understanding of a range of ethical and religious issues surrounding abortion
- debate the choices that those involved in decision-making realistically have.

- **Look at the following illustrations.**
- **Which do you agree with most and why?**

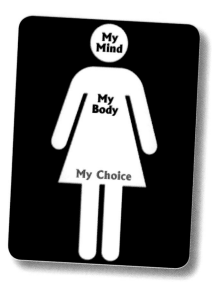

Whose choice should it be concerning the issue of abortion?

Abortion is a difficult decision for anyone to make and could be made for a variety of reasons:

- the person(s) involved may be considered too young to make responsible parents
- they may not have enough money to support a child
- this may not be the right point in their careers to have children
- the foetus may have an abnormality
- the child could be the result of a one-night stand.

Whose decision should it be? Should it be the decision of the pregnant woman? The father of the foetus? The parents of the pregnant woman? The doctor?

Activities

1 Work in pairs. For each situation on the list above, try to decide who should make the decision concerning abortion.

2 Write a speech either in favour of, or against, abortion. In it, you must show you have considered both points of view and why you have rejected one. You must also refer to the teaching of the Christian Church and why you accept or reject it.

Sacred texts

JEWISH AND CHRISTIAN
Thou shalt not kill.

Exodus 20:13 – The Ten Commandments

You created every part of me; you put me together in my mother's womb.

Psalm 139:13

Naked I came from my mother's womb, and naked shall I return; the Lord gave, and the Lord has taken away; blessed be the name of the Lord.

Job 1:21

In his hand is the life of every living thing and the breath of all mankind.

Job 12:10

SIKH
In the first watch of the night, O my merchant friend, you were cast into the womb, by the Lord's Command. Upside-down, within the womb, you performed penance, O my merchant friend, and you prayed to your Lord and Master… As God's Pen has written on your forehead, so it shall be with your soul.

Adi Granth 74

Question

Explain the teachings from two religious traditions about abortion. *(6 mark question, AO1)*

Level 1

First, make sure that you have made a relevant statement about a teaching from two religious traditions. For example, 'Christians have differing views on abortion. Some allow it, but some don't. Most Jews are against abortion.'

Level 2

Then, explain the teaching from the two religious traditions. For example, 'Roman Catholic Christians are not allowed abortions under any circumstances, because they believe that all life is a gift from God so should be preserved. Most Jews don't allow abortion because the Torah states 'Thou shalt not kill', which means that it is wrong to kill under any circumstances, including abortion.'

Level 3

Next, give a deeper explanation of the teachings of the two religious traditions. Try to bring in religious language. For example, 'Roman Catholics believe in the "sanctity of life", which means that all life is holy and sacred. Only God has the right to end life, so abortion is wrong. Most Jews would also be against abortion, because they believe that all life is God-given so must be preserved and valued.'

Level 4

Finally, draw together your ideas. Make sure that your answer shows good understanding of the main teachings from the two religious traditions. Use religious language extensively. For example, 'Not all Christians are against abortion. Some Protestants are "pro-choice" and believe that the rights of the mother are important, too. They wouldn't allow an abortion for social reasons, but would allow it if it was a choice between the mother's health and the birth of the child. Some Jews, particularly Progressive or Reform Jews, may allow a woman to have an abortion if she has been raped or if her health was at risk.'

Must think about!

At the moment, the father of a foetus has no legal rights. A woman may have an abortion without his knowledge or consent, even if the couple is married. What do you think about this?

2.7 Euthanasia (1)

The next two pages will help you to:

- explain what is meant by euthanasia and compare the different types
- debate the sensitive issue of whether it is ever right, from a religious or ethical point of view, to take someone's life.

- Should people be helped to die?
- Is there such as thing as a 'mercy killing'?

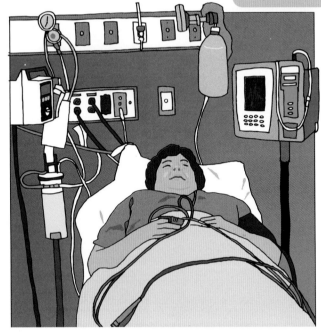

A person being kept alive on a life-support machine

Activities

1 In your opinion, which (if any) of the forms of euthanasia are acceptable?

2 Find out about the case of Diane Pretty, who wanted the right to end her life. Should she have been allowed this right?

3 In small groups, try to come up with at least two arguments for and two against euthanasia. Record them in a 'For' and 'Against' chart. Leave space to add more arguments.

Whose life is it anyway?

The end of life is an important time for both the person who is dying and their family and friends. But who has the right to say when death should actually come? Should the dying person, their family or the medical profession decide that death should take place in a particular way? It may not seem to be the correct thing to do to prolong a person's life at all costs, and there is the question of human dignity and quality of life. This is why euthanasia has become a contentious issue and why religious teaching has much to say on the subject.

What is euthanasia?

Euthanasia comes from Greek words meaning 'gentle death' or 'good death'. Some people call it 'mercy killing'.

There are four kinds of euthanasia:

- Voluntary euthanasia – where the person asks to be helped to die.
- Involuntary euthanasia – where, for example, ethnic cleansing takes place.
- Active euthanasia – where a specific action takes place to end the person's life, such as an overdose of tablets.
- Passive euthanasia – where life-supporting treatment is removed.

Doctors and nurses are not allowed to advise on whether the patient should be allowed euthanasia.

I will neither give a deadly drug to anybody who asked for it, nor will I make a suggestion to this effect.
Hippocratic Oath

What do the different religions teach on euthanasia?

Judaism teaching

Jews are opposed to euthanasia. Judaism teaches that all life is a precious gift. It is not ours to throw away should we wish to do so. Only the Creator should decide when a life should end. Pain-relief medicine can be given to Jews, even though it may hasten death. However, it is important that the dose is certain not to kill, and that the intention is not to kill, but to relieve pain.

Some Jews believe that people who need a life-support machine to keep them alive, and have no realistic chance of recovery, should be allowed to die. Doctors should not make a person suffer more by artificially extending their life, but equally they should not hasten death.

It is acceptable to pray to end a person's pain and suffering. It is wrong to shorten a life even if it would end very soon. Every moment of human life is considered equal in value to many years of life.

Active euthanasia is seen as murder.

Christian teaching

Generally, Christians are opposed to euthanasia. The timing of a person's death should be left to God. All human life is seen as sacred, and belonging to God, therefore to take it away – whatever the circumstances – is unacceptable.

Whatever else it is, euthanasia is ultimately taking a life, which is expressly forbidden. Some would argue that turning off a life-support machine, when it is not possible for there to be independent existence, is not wrong, but what love and compassion requires.

Hospices are available to cope with death in a positive and meaningful way.

Sikhism teaching

Most Sikhs are against euthanasia. They believe that the timing of birth and death should be left in God's hands and human beings should not feel that they have the right to end it. However, in the case of prolonging life by artificial means and putting a person through unnecessary suffering, the close relatives have the right to decide.

Sikhs have a high respect for life, which is seen as a gift from God. The Sikh Gurus rejected suicide (and, by extension, euthanasia) as an interference in God's plan. Suffering is part of the operation of *karma*. Human beings should not only accept it without complaint, but act so as to make the best of the situation that *karma* has given them. Suffering is part of the human condition and it has a place in the scheme of God.

Sikhs contemplating euthanasia for themselves or others should look at the whole picture in order to make appropriate distinctions between ending life and not artificially prolonging a terminal state. Caring is considered more important.

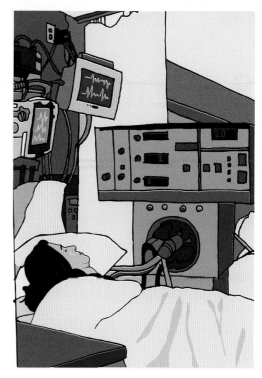

Is turning off a life-support machine the same as killing someone?

Activities

4 Read the teachings of Christianity and at least one other religious tradition again. Summarise their teachings and add their teachings in the correct place in a 'For' and 'Against' chart.

5 Read the following case study.

Case study

Jessica is a Roman Catholic Christian. She has a terminal illness and has become reliant on family to care for her. She feels that she has no dignity any more. Jessica's beliefs mean that she cannot request euthanasia.

Try to advise Jessica on other things that she can do to alleviate her suffering without resorting to euthanasia.

2.8 Euthanasia (2)

Must think about!

Here are some questions to consider.

■ Should people who are sick be allowed to end their lives?

■ If they are going to die anyway, does it matter?

■ How far should the wishes of the next of kin be considered, especially if they are likely to gain from the death?

■ How far should the quality of life be considered?

■ If the patient were a pet animal, would we do the same thing?

Is it ever right to end someone's life?

Non-treatment (passive euthanasia) is not the same as killing the person, nor is switching off a life-support machine when the person is apparently dependent on it. For example, Karen Ann Quinlan fell into a coma in April 1975. She was placed on a respirator and a feeding tube for about a year, before her family asked for the machines to be turned off. They were finally granted permission from the New Jersey Supreme Court in the USA to remove Karen from life support in 1976; amazingly, she lived on in a coma until she died of pneumonia in 1985!

Situations like these make people question whether we have the right to end someone's life. Some people, particularly religious believers, would say that only God can make the decision about when life should end.

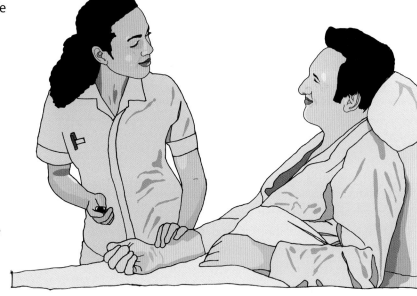

Some people see hospices as an alternative to euthanasia

What are the alternatives?

Drug therapy, hospitalisation, psychiatric treatment, physiotherapy and palliative care are all considered alternatives to euthanasia when someone is extremely unwell. Many argue that these can still offer quality of life to the patient and prevent them from being a burden.

The work of a hospice

There is a common belief that a hospice is where everyone goes to die. That is not true. The average stay in a hospice is 12 to 14 days, after which many patients return home.

During their stay, patients will receive treatment (known as palliative care) to help relieve pain and other symptoms causing discomfort. They will also receive a great deal of love, care and skilled attention from trained medical, nursing and support staff.

Hospice patients can be any age, from a tiny baby to the very old. Some 80 per cent of patients will have cancer, but the remaining 20 per cent will be suffering from a wide variety of illnesses for which hospice expertise can make a difference. Hospices were originally resting places for the weary traveller; they still are. But more, they add quality and dignity to the lives of those who visit, ensuring that, if required, the remainder of the journey is not undertaken alone. (National Association of Hospice Fundraisers)

Activities

1   Look at the following pictures of hospices. What impression of hospices to you get from them?

2   Read the following list. In your opinion, should any of the examples be allowed euthanasia? Give reasons for your answers.
   - A person suffering from severe arthritis who cannot walk properly and is in pain.
   - A person suffering from AIDS.
   - A person with terminal cancer.
   - A person suffering from depression.

Research note

Find out which countries allow euthanasia.

Try to find out why it is not allowed in Britain.

2.9 IVF

■ Do you know how people can overcome infertility?

■ Look at the following chart. What does it tell you about how age and pregnancy are related?

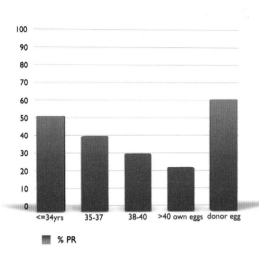

Pregnancy success rates by age group

Is it right to spend so much money on IVF when people are starving in the world?

Unfortunately, science has shown that the ability to become pregnant decreases with age. These days, women are leaving it until much later than earlier generations to start a family. Women are often eager to pursue a career or to be financially stable, before they begin trying to have children. Sometimes people find that, by the time they are ready for a family, they cannot conceive naturally.

There are also occasions when men and women cannot conceive naturally for many other reasons, such as a low sperm count or a 'hostile' womb.

But did you know that the average cost of one attempt at IVF is between £4,000 and £8,000? It is also debatable whether the money for this should be paid by the NHS, or whether that money could be better spent elsewhere.

What is IVF?

In vitro fertilisation (IVF) is a process in which egg cells are fertilised by sperm outside the woman's womb, *in vitro*. IVF has made major advances. Other methods of overcoming infertility are:
■ AIH – artificial insemination using the husband's/partner's sperm
■ AID – artificial insemination using sperm from a donor
■ surrogacy – another woman carrying a child in her womb for the couple
■ adoption – bringing up a child from a different family
■ egg donation – using an egg donated by another woman.

Apart from the cost, sometimes people are against fertility treatment, because they feel that it may cause identity issues for the child born as a result. The following could happen in real life.
■ A couple is unable to conceive naturally.
■ A sperm donor donates sperm for the couple.
■ An egg donor donates an egg for the couple.
■ A surrogate mother carries the child in her womb from conception.

These prompt the questions: Who are the child's parents? What issues might arise as the child grows up?

Must think about!

Did you know?

In 2005, a law was passed stating that sperm donors can no longer remain anonymous.

■ What issues might this cause?
■ Why do you think this law was felt to be necessary?

What do the religions teach on IVF?

Christian teaching on IVF

Roman Catholics

- The Roman Catholic Church is opposed to most kinds of IVF and teaches that infertility is a call from God to adopt children.
- IVF 'infringes the child's right to be born of a father and mother known to him and bound to each other by marriage.' (*Catechism of the Catholic Church*)
- Roman Catholics (and many other Christian denominations) see embryos as human lives with the same rights as all other lives. Spare embryos are destroyed during IVF and therefore IVF is unacceptable.
- God intended conception to be the result of sexual intercourse.

Anglicans

- The Church of England states that the use of embryos until they are 14 days old is acceptable.
- The Church also allows sperm and egg donation, arguing that this is the same as adopting a child.
- Paid surrogacy, however, is not allowed.
- Some Christians believe that IVF is a good idea because it brings happiness and children to couples who would otherwise have been childless.

Judaism teaching on IVF

- There is no problem with destroying spare embryos, as the Talmud (rabbinic discussions on Jewish Law) states that the soul does not enter the embryo until it is 40 days old.
- Jews believe that they have an obligation to have children and to 'be fruitful and multiply'. (*Genesis 1:22*) IVF is therefore obligatory if it is medically advised as a way for a couple to have children.
- If an egg is donated to a couple, it has to be from a Jewish woman.
- Israel is a world leader in fertility treatments. It is the only country that pays for infertile couples to have two babies.

Sikhism teaching on IVF

- Sikhs believe that it is desirable for married couples to have children, because they will look after their parents in old age.
- If a couple cannot conceive naturally, fertility treatments such as AIH and IVF are allowed, providing the egg and sperm are those of the same couple.
- Surrogacy is not allowed as it would be seen as a form of adultery.
- Like some Christians, Sikhs see IVF as a gift from God, to be used to bring happiness to childless couples who cannot conceive on their own.

Activity

1 Create a spider diagram OR a Venn diagram showing the religious teachings of Christianity and at least one other religious tradition about IVF.

GradeStudio

Question

Explain how having a religious faith might influence someone making a choice about whether to have IVF? *(4 mark question, AO1)*

Level 1

First, make a simple link between what religious believers might do and why. For example, 'Having religious faith might help a believer, because they might pray to God for advice about IVF.'

Level 2

Next, make sure that you have explained WHY a religious believer might do these things. For example, 'A believer may find it useful to pray because there are no teachings about IVF in their holy books.'

Level 3

Then, show awareness of other ways in which having faith can help a believer to make a decision. For example, 'A religious believer may follow the teachings of their tradition when making a decision about IVF. They might look in their holy books for guidance or speak to a leader.'

Level 4

Finally, make sure that your answer shows understanding of religious practices and reasons for them. Include religious language. For example, 'A Jew might read the passage in Genesis that says "Be fruitful and multiply", and interpret this as meaning that they should have lots of children, so IVF is acceptable.'

2 Religion and medicine
Remember and Reflect

The questions in this section are based on the work you have done throughout this topic. Try to complete as many as you can.

The questions in set 1 are designed to test your factual recall and AO1 level skills (knowledge and understanding). The page numbers alongside the questions will help you to find information that might be useful for your answers. Use them to check against what you have written.

The questions in set 2 are more challenging, using AO2 level skills (use of evidence and reasoned argument to evaluate personal responses and differing viewpoints). Your answers may come from more than one part of the topic.

Set 1

1	Explain the meaning of the following terms:
	  a sanctity of life
	  b Hippocratic Oath
	  c medical ethics.
		pages 40–41

2	Give two reasons why a religious believer would say that life is special.	**pages 42–43**
3	Recall a religious quotation that shows that life is special.	**pages 42–43**
4	What areas of medicine come under the heading 'medical ethics'?	**pages 46–49**
5	State three ways in which a religious believer can make a decision about medical ethics.	**pages 46–49**
6	State five body parts that can be transplanted.	**pages 44–45**

7 Which of the following religious traditions would not allow abortion under any circumstances? pages 46–49
Try to give a reason why.

   a Roman Catholic

   b Anglican

   c Orthodox Jew

   d Sikh

8 How many types of euthanasia are there? Try to list them. pages 54–55

9 Explain two reasons why most religious believers are against euthanasia. pages 54–57

10 Choose two religious traditions. Write three of their teachings about IVF. pages 58–59

11 List three types of fertility treatment. pages 58–59

Set 2

Answer the following questions in as much detail as possible.

12 When do you think that life begins? Explain your reasons.

   a At conception

   b When the foetus's heart beats

   c When the foetus is fully developed

   d At birth

13 Do you think that euthanasia should be allowed? Try to consider more than one point of view.

14 Do you think that cloning is a good idea or a bad idea? Explain your reasons.

15 *'Life and death should be left to God.'* Choose two religious traditions. Explain their arguments for and against this statement.

16 As a class, debate the following statement: *'Medicine has got out of hand.'*

17 Draw an opinion line in your book. Place the following medical procedures on the line according to your views on them:

   a genetic engineering

   b euthanasia

   c abortion

   d IVF

   e organ donation.

OK ⊢————————————————————⊣ NOT OK

GradeStudio

On these pages you will find the types of question you might encounter in the exam, along with sample answers and comments. A good understanding of this information may help you to improve the content and structure of your own answers.

You may wish to refer to the level descriptor grids in the Introduction (pages 10–11).

Question

'If people can't have children, they should just accept it, not waste time with IVF.' Do you agree? Give reasons or evidence for your answer, showing that you have thought of more than one point of view. You must include reference to religious beliefs in your answer.　　**(8 mark question, AO2)**

Student's answer

Some people might agree with this because they think that everything happens for a reason. Maybe God doesn't want them to have children. Other people might disagree because they see it as their right to have children. **(Level 1)** The Creation story in Genesis tells Christians and Jews that they should have children. **(Level 2)**

Comments

The student gave a clear point of view along with a reason for this view, and also referred briefly to another point of view. This puts the answer at Level 1. The student then went on to give a religious teaching to support the second viewpoint, which earned Level 2. To reach Level 3, the student would have to explain both points of view in more detail, referring to religious or moral ideas about the statement for each point of view. To reach Level 4, they would need to thoroughly discuss the idea of IVF and religious attitudes towards it, including a range of religious teachings to support their arguments

Student's improved answer

Some people might agree with this, because they think that everything happens for a reason. Maybe God doesn't want them to have children. Roman Catholics believe that infertility may be God's call for the couple to adopt, therefore they shouldn't attempt IVF. Catholics also have a problem with IVF because unused embryos are thrown way, which is like throwing away a life, which comes from God.

Other people might disagree because they see it as their right to have children. The Creation story in Genesis tells Christians and Jews that they should have children. **(Level 3)** Jews see it as their duty to have children, so therefore IVF is acceptable. Some Christians would also disagree with the statement because they think that God has given them the knowledge to perform IVF. Also, IVF can produce a child who would bring happiness to the couple. **(Level 4)**

Question

'Only God has the right to end life.' Give two reasons why a religious believer might agree or disagree with the statement.
(4 mark question, AO2)

Level 1	A simple, appropriate justification of a point of view.
Level 2	Either: an expanded justification of one point of view, with appropriate example and /or illustration, which includes religious teaching. Or: two simple, appropriate justifications of a point of view.
Level 3	An expanded justification of one point of view, with appropriate example and/or illustration, which includes religious teaching, with a second simple appropriate justification of a point of view (which may be an alternative to the first)
Level 4	An expanded justification of two viewpoints, incorporating the religious teachings and moral aspects at issue and their implications for the individual and the rest of society.

Student's answer

Some religious believers might agree with the statement because they think all life is a gift from God so they must respect it. (Level 1)

Other religious believers might disagree because they think God gave us free will to make our own decisions. (Level 2)

Comments

The student gives a simple justification of a point of view, which earns Level 1. The student then makes another simple justification of a point of view, which earns Level 2. To reach Level 3, the student should expand the points of view to include religious teachings. To reach Level 4, the student should explain the religious teachings and moral aspects of the issue in more detail.

Student's improved answer

Some religious believers might agree with the statement because they think all life is a gift from God, so they must respect it. (Level 1) A Christian might refer to the idea of the 'sanctity of life' to show that all life is precious, so we must not end life. (Level 2)

Other religious believers might disagree because they think God gave us free will to make our own decisions. (Level 3) When Adam and Eve were created, they were given free will. This might mean that ending a life is our decision. (Level 4)

3 Religious expression

The Big Picture

- In this topic you will be addressing religious issues about expressing one's faith.
- This topic covers three principal religions: Christianity, Judaism and Hinduism.
- You will need to focus on least two principal religions.

You will look at:

- how faith is expressed through actions – the work of religious charities and organisations
- how faith is expressed through what can be worn
- how faith is expressed through symbols in places of worship
- how faith is expressed through pilgrimage
- how faith is expressed through sharing faith with others.

You will also think about the ways in which faith can influence the actions and behaviour of religious believers and how they affect the life of a believer in today's society.

What?

You will:

- examine religious beliefs, practices, values and traditions about the way faith is expressed
- develop your knowledge and understanding of the strong connection that exists between faith and how a believer lives their life
- consider human experiences and issues and look at specific examples of how faith is expressed
- determine your own attitudes and opinions towards how faith may be expressed.

Why?

Because:

- these issues will allow you to explore your own beliefs and allow you to understand why religious believers may want to share their faith with others
- you will recognise and value the religious beliefs of others
- considering how individuals and faith communities express their religious faith in contemporary society will give you a balanced view of religion
- understanding a range of attitudes will help you to see how and why some people are motivated to act because of their religious beliefs.

How?

By:

- using knowledge and understanding to describe how religious believers express their faith
- using knowledge and understanding to explain why religious believers express their faith
- using evidence and argument to analyse different opinions, including your own views about these issues.

1 On your own, answer as many of the questions as possible. Try to give detailed responses.

   a) Write down three words that you think describe you.

   b) Write down three words to describe how you think others may see you.

   c) Write down one item that you wear that you feel expresses you (it may be an item of clothing or a piece of jewellery, etc.)

   d) Draw a symbol that you feel represents what you are like. Write a short explanation of it.

   e) Is there a place that is special to you? Where is it and why is it so special?

   f) Give an example of something you do with others that shows you have something in common (for example, support a football team, go shopping together).

2 Now share your ideas with a partner.

   a) Did they agree with how you described yourself?

   b) Which questions did you find more challenging to answer and why was this?

   c) Did religion feature in any of your answers? Explain why it did or didn't.

   d) Do you feel it is important that you express who you are and what you are like? Why or why not?

   e) How do you feel a religious believer may have answered the questions? Would their responses have been very different from yours?

Develop Your Knowledge

This topic is about expressing one's faith. Read the information below, which will help you to think about the issues before you begin more detailed work.

Key information

- Faith and religious belief can provide a purpose in life, involving helping others through charities and organisations.

- Charities such as Christian Aid, Tzedek and Hindu Aid are religious organisations that attempt to bring justice to the world and end poverty.

- Many religious believers feel it is important to express themselves and their faith through the objects that they wear.

- There is some debate about whether religious believers really need to make their faith explicit.

- Art is a form of expression and it helps to point to the deeper meanings of religion or allows believers to express their beliefs.

- Holy buildings have symbols within them, which are helpful or conducive to worship.

- Pilgrimages are special journeys that religious believers go on.

- Some people argue that pilgrimage is out of date today.

- One method of expressing faith is through sharing it with others.

- The media is an important tool in representing religion.

Key words

*community a group of people who are joined together, because they share something in common

*evangelism spreading a faith or religion to others

*faith to have trust or confidence

*identity the sense of who you are in terms of attitudes, character and personality

injustice when things are unfair and humans rights are denied; when everything is not equal

long-term aid help that is intended to last for a long time, such as helping people to become self-sufficient

*pilgrimage a form of spiritual adventure

*sacred something to be revered or respected above other things

short-term aid help given to those who need it immediately after a disaster to ensure they can survive

*We draw attention to these key words in particular because they are the ones that appear in the WJEC specification.

Key questions

- Can a religion give a purpose in life?
- Why do people support others?
- How can a belief drive actions?
- How can faith be expressed through what people wear?
- Do religious believers need to make their faith explicit?
- How can art express one's faith?
- Why worship in special buildings?
- What makes a place conducive to worship?
- What makes a journey special?
- Can pilgrimage help a person's spiritual growth?
- Is pilgrimage out of date?
- Is there a purpose or value to interfaith dialogue?
- Is it right for people to share their faith with others?
- How should the media be used for religious purposes?

For interest

There are a huge number of ways to express yourself and your beliefs. Banksy is a famous graffiti artist who chooses to represent politics, culture and ethics through street graffiti. This is a form of expression.

How is this image a form of expression?

Important questions

- How do you express yourself? Is it through what you wear, how you speak, how you behave?
- Do you have an original method of allowing people to understand you or see the 'real you'?

3.1 The work of religious charities and organisations

- **Have you ever helped someone who was in need?**
- **What was it that you did?**
- **Why did you help them?**

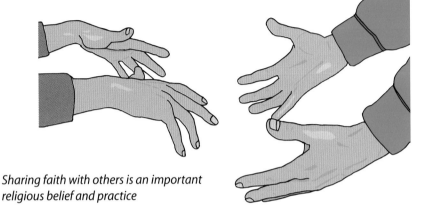

Sharing faith with others is an important religious belief and practice

Can a religion give a purpose in life?

It is faith that gives meaning and purpose to the lives of religious believers. The term **faith** means trust or confidence. For religious believers it means to have a trust or confidence in God. It is this that helps to create their **identity** and gives a sense of purpose to who they are.

A religious faith gives direction to people's lives. Many religious believers belong to a local community, regularly attending a place of worship, which is an expression of faith.

Many religious believers also choose to spend some of their own personal time involved in charity work. Part of the expression of a religious faith is to want to help other people. Some people simply give money to street collections or donate money in collection envelopes. Some may buy charity Christmas cards or give up time to work in a local charity shop. Charity is about helping other people who are in need.

Activities

1 What do you know about religious charities? Make a list of ideas individually and then share your ideas with others. Try to think about what work charities do, what the aims of charities are and who charities try to help.

2 As a class, list all the charities you can think of. Try to categorise them into local charities and global charities. Try to identify which religions they are associated with.

3 Create a concept map using words and pictures to show the reasons why Christians, Jews and Hindus believe it is important to help others. Try to colour code ideas to identify which religion they belong to.

4 Do you think it is always possible for religious believers to help and support others? Explain at least three reasons for your answer.

How do religious charities or organisations help?

Consider the following examples.

Christian Aid
- Wants to create and establish a world free from poverty and injustice.
- Provides relief in times of disaster and helps people regardless of religion or nationality.
- Speaks out against injustice.
- Tries to deliver real, practical help where it is most needed.
- Campaigns for change.

Tzedek
- Is a Jewish overseas development and educational charity.
- Works with some of the poorest people in the world, regardless of their race or religion.
- Tries to help people in distress and in damaging political and economic conditions.
- Helps to fund small-scale, self-help sustainable projects, assisting people long term in looking after themselves and coping with the conditions they live in.

HINDU AID
Hindu Aid
- Is an organisation that helps the work of Hindu organisations in the UK.
- Focuses particularly on projects, including education, removing poverty, providing relief after natural disasters and helping those needing water or medical care.
- Bases its ideas on the concepts of serving, sharing and caring, which are contained in their holy scriptures.

Research note
- Find out what other work charity organisations do? Research CAFOD, Tearfund and any others you know of.
- Famous names have often supported religious charities or organisations. Alan Sugar isn't religious, but supports Jewish Care, while Cliff Richard 'tithes' (meaning he gives a percentage of his annual income to charity). Dermot O'Leary has completed charity work for CAFOD. See what you can find out about other famous people who have supported religious charities and organisations.

Activities
5. Do you think short-term or long-term aid is more successful? Why?

6. Research one religious organisation and identify what work they do that comes under short-term aid and what work they do that comes under long-term aid. Create a poster or presentation showing this information.

Why do people support others?

Being compassionate and caring about other people is an important aspect of being a religious believer. Christians follow the example of Jesus, who spent much time helping others. Jews have similar beliefs to Christians, claiming that God wants us to help each other, because we were all made in his image and are all worthy of care. Hindus believe every living thing is valuable and put this teaching into practice by supporting others.

How can a belief drive actions?

Religious beliefs drive the actions of individuals who try to make a difference in the world. Many organisations are involved with short-term and long-term aid to help those in need.

Short-term aid means responding to emergency requests as a result of famine, war and natural disasters. Usually this means food, water, shelter and medical assistance.

Long-term aid requires more structure, providing technology for clean drinking water, sanitation, sustainable farming methods, education and employment.

For debate
'*Does a charity need to be linked to a religion to be effective?*' Think about your own views on this question. Try to make a table, showing the arguments 'For' and 'Against' this. What do you think religious believers would argue and why?

3.2 Expressing faith through what is worn (1)

The next two pages will help you to:

- examine examples of how faith can be expressed through what people wear
- explore some of the debates that have taken place over the wearing of religious symbols.

- Is there something you wear to express your personality? For example, Goths often dress in black or people who enjoy fitness may dress in tracksuits. Their clothes or items reflect the person they are or the beliefs they hold.

- How do religious believers try to express their faith through what they wear?

How are these items expressions of faith?

How can faith be expressed through what people wear?

Religious dress is just one of the ways in which religious believers may express their faith. It may be part of the identity of a religious faith or part of the culture. It may involve wearing special clothes or special objects. In a multicultural society, there are many examples to choose from.

Activities

1 Compile a list of special clothes or objects that are worn by religious believers. Try to identify why they are worn and which religion they belong to.

2 Read this news article about a teenager living in Britain. This is not a real example, but there are many sorts of similar cases. Try to find out more about these, for example wearing a chastity ring, Sikh bracelet or Islamic hijab at school.

3 The article above raises a number of questions about religious expression in schools. What do you think? Should pupils be allowed to wear objects of religion at school? What religions should be included in this? What about religious dress? Are there health and safety issues in subjects such as physical education and practical subjects?

Banned from expressing her religion

A 14-year-old schoolgirl has been banned from expressing her faith at school. She wanted to wear her crucifix on a chain around her neck under her uniform, but the school rules forbid the wearing of jewellery. When asked to remove the item, she refused and was immediately excluded by the head teacher. When asked, he argued that his hands were tied as 'no jewellery' was a school rule. He felt he was unable to make an exception, even though the item was not physically visible. The matter has not been resolved and the girl involved remains excluded from the school, until she consents to follow all the school rules.

4 Prepare a speech to present at your school council to argue your point of view and try to convince others that you are right. You need to address each of the questions above. Try to use evidence to justify your point of view; you may need to do further research.

Should religious believers be allowed to express their faith in whatever way they want?

Many religious believers claim that expressing their faith through the wearing of certain clothes or religious objects is essential to their faith. Objectors argue that faith is a personal thing and it doesn't state in all religions that these objects should be worn.

How can we identify which religion someone belongs to by what they are wearing?

It is often easy to identify which faith someone belongs to. There are sometimes obvious signs that we can interpret to help us.

Activities

5   Analyse the people in this picture. See if you can…

  a   state the name of the religion of each person
  b   state the name of the religious object(s) being worn
  c   describe any form of religious dress
  d   explain why the object or form of dress is important: What does it symbolise? And why is it being worn?

6   a   Create your own list of the ways in which religious believers can show to or share their faith with others. Use the ideas above to get started. Try to categorise your ideas by showing which religious tradition they belong to.

   b   Which of the ideas on your list do you think are most effective in expressing the faith of a believer? Why do you think this?

Answers to Activities 5a and b

Sikh girl with a kara bangle.
Christian girl with a cross around her neck.
Jewish boy with a prayer shawl and kippah.
Jewish man with a kippah and phylacteries.
Hindu girl with a tilak spot on her forehead.

How do religious believers make their faith explicit?

Religious believers feel it is important to show and share their faith with others. This can take a variety of forms, from simply wearing something that defines their religion, to talking to people about their faith, to demonstrating their religious beliefs by refusing to do something.

Some ways of expressing faith could be:
- wearing a crucifix or cross
- preaching and teaching others about religious beliefs
- not working on a holy day
- making a decision not to have sex before marriage
- going on a pilgrimage to Jerusalem.

3.3 Expressing faith through what is worn (2)

The next two pages will help you to:

■ explore why some religious believers need to make their faith explicit.

■ Faith is an important part of life for a religious believer. For many, it is something that affects everything they do, every action and every decision they make. Why do you think this is the case for religious believers?

■ Have you ever been in the challenging position of not being able to do something, because it doesn't 'fit' with your faith or beliefs?

Do religious believers need to make their faith explicit?

The question whether or not it is necessary for religious believers to make their faith explicit needs to be addressed. Sometimes others may find what they are doing offensive or intrusive.

Why do religious believers feel it is important to make their faith explicit?

Some religions teach that it is vital to share their religion with others. Religious believers feel it is important that other people have access to their faith, so they can make an informed decision. Others feel that faith is such an important part of their lives that they want to show it to others or they want physical reminders of their faith. For some, displaying their faith is a way of identifying themselves. This is particularly important if living in a country where their religion is in a minority. It is a way of showing what they believe and identifying themselves to others – both those who share similar beliefs and those who don't. It can reduce the possibility of offending others or being disrespectful accidentally.

Activity

1 Read the information opposite and then answer the questions that follow:

a What dilemmas did Eric Liddell, Harold Abrahams and Jonathan Edwards face and what action did they take?

b Why do you think Eric Liddell and Jonathan Edwards decided not to take part in their sports on Sundays? What things may they have taken into consideration?

c Explain in your own words what you think may have changed Jonathan Edwards' mind.

d Why do you think Harold Abrahams took a different position?

Chariots of Fire was a film made in 1981 and features the true story of two British athletes competing in the 1924 Olympics in Paris. Eric Liddell was a devout Christian, who expressed his religious beliefs by refusing to run his heat on a Sunday. Instead, he changed events so that his sport didn't conflict with his religious beliefs. This is one example of someone putting their religious beliefs first. The other athlete, Harold Abrahams, was Jewish and admitted he was driven to achieve his dream because of the increase in anti-Semitism. He was therefore inspired by this to win, although he later converted to Roman Catholicism.

Today, these men could be compared to someone such as Jonathan Edwards, the British triple jumper, who initially refused to compete on Sundays as it was against his Christian faith. He found a different compromise, however, as he came to see his ability in sports as a gift from God and believed he should use it, regardless of the day of the week.

Many people choose to make their faith explicit. They may feel that otherwise it is ignored or not understood by others. Some may even feel that they want to be true to themselves and expressing their faith is a way for them to do this.

Activity

2 **a** Look at the statements below. Create a table with three columns, showing whether they are *supporting* the idea of making faith explicit, *not supporting* it or are *neutral*. Add any other ideas that you can think of.

> Wearing something that reflects my faith reminds me of its importance in my daily life.

> I don't see why people need reminders of their faith – shouldn't faith be internal not external?

> Religious symbols can be scary – the women wearing hijab in Islam make some people uncomfortable.

> It can be difficult at school to wear school uniform as it's not how we want to express ourselves – why should it be different for religious believers?

> I don't have a problem with believers showing their faith, as long as they don't inflict their beliefs on me.

> If religious believers are allowed to share their beliefs, I should be allowed to dress how I want to express my beliefs and ideas.

> I want to share my faith with others so they understand my beliefs.

> An important part of my religion is to spread the word of God.

b Add one more idea of your own to each column.

c Using the ideas from the previous activity, create a response to the question *'Do you think that religious believers need to express their faith?'*

d Share your ideas with a partner and then create an answer together, showing what religious believers would argue and why.

Question

'Religious believers should not have to wear symbols of their faith.' Give two reasons why a religious believer might agree or disagree. *(1 mark question, AO2)*

Levels will be used to measure the quality of your response (AO2). A good answer will explain instead of simply describing why religious believers may hold different views. Try to show how it links to other beliefs.

Level 1

First, offer a simple explanation of a view. For example, refer to the fact that many religious believers claim it is important to show their beliefs and commitment.

Level 2

Develop your answer by referring to examples or religious teachings. For example, 'Christians believe wearing a crucifix or cross reminds them of their faith and demonstrates it to others.'

Level 3

Ensure that you give two separate reasons, showing your understanding of other evidence, such as the fact that others may disagree, because sometimes it is inappropriate to wear certain items.

Level 4

Conclude your answer by making sure you have given sufficient explanation. For example, explain that it may not be appropriate or safe in some circumstances, for example in science laboratories or in some jobs where objects may not be suitable for the duties involved. Also, there may be occasions where it would be disrespectful, such as if you were of a different religion and entered a Christian church wearing the clothes and symbols of another religion. Christians could take offence at your lack of respect.

3.4 Expressing faith through symbols in a place of worship

The next two pages will help you to:

- identify how faith can be expressed through works of art
- identify symbols in places of worship and how these express faith.

- Images can be very powerful. They can help someone to concentrate on a single idea or even express their own beliefs, views or feelings about something. If you were asked to represent yourself in art, what would you produce and why?

Do you recognise these famous images. How do they express faith?

How can art express one's faith?

Art may be used to provide a visual focus for the worshipper or allow artists themselves to express their faith. Religious art has a long history, with many images being produced in various forms to display key ideas and beliefs or to tell stories. Christianity, Judaism and Hinduism are all religions that are steeped in stories and imagery that convey special meanings. Art is often seen as symbolic or metaphorical and can be interpreted by religious believers. Many stories from **sacred** texts are more understandable when conveyed in pictorial form. Art is a form of expression in itself, but is a useful tool, conveying deeper meanings than language alone. Art can also provide a focus for worshippers to meditate on, so they can feel closer to their faith and religion.

Research note

Find five examples of religious art that show different aspects of faith. How do they do this?

Activities

1   Look at the art images at the top of the page. What can you see? In what ways do you think they provide a focus for the worshipper? Try to write five sentences on each artwork.

2   Using the information above, make a list of ways in which art can be used to express faith.

How do symbols help?

Holy buildings may be of a special design and may contain images that help people to worship and express faith. Symbolism is found in most places of worship, including those of the Christian church, the Jewish synagogue and the Hindu temple (mandir). These signs or symbols are an expression of some aspect of religious belief. Symbols help to create and maintain a sense of religious identity.

Christianity

A cross or crucifix expresses religious beliefs about Jesus Christ. In some Protestant churches, the cross is a symbol of the death of Jesus, although the cross is empty to express the belief that Jesus is resurrected. In the Roman Catholic tradition, there is more of an emphasis on the death and suffering of Jesus, so the crucifix, a cross with a figure of Jesus, is more common. In the Orthodox tradition, icons (images) depicting the death of Jesus on the cross are an integral part of the decoration.

You might see a cross on the church noticeboard, fixed to the outside of the building, or in a graveyard on headstones. Inside, a cross or crucifix would be used at the front as a focal point. The symbols may be used in paintings, on church banners or in stained-glass windows. Priests may wear vestments that display a variety of religious symbols, including the cross. Christians may also choose to wear a cross or crucifix on a chain as a symbol of their religious belief and commitment. Roman Catholics may carry a rosary to help them recite prayers, but also as a sign of their faith. Sometimes you will see a rosary hanging from a car mirror. The Ichthus is also a common sign of Christianity.

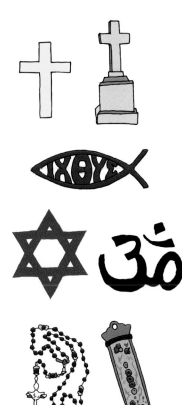

Judaism

The *mezuzah* placed on an outside doorpost is an expression of religious belief. It is also a religious artefact. In religion, these artefacts frequently have a symbolic value as well as a practical use. In any synagogue, Orthodox or Reform, there will be a variety of symbols used both to express religious belief and to help worship. The *ner tamid* (eternal flame) is an expression of the belief that God is present today, and a reminder of the past when there was a flame burning in the *menorah* in the Temple at Jerusalem. In the same way in which Christians may choose to wear a symbol of their faith, it is important to understand that Jews may also choose to wear symbols as part of their faith, such as a *kippah*, *tallit*, *tefillin* and *Magen David*. It is also important to understand that symbols may be worn in public, in a place of worship or privately.

Hinduism

The Hindu mandir contains symbolism and many examples of expressions of faith. Usually brightly coloured and featuring statues and images of the Hindu gods and goddesses, it is a holy building dedicated to the act of worship. Artefacts such as the puja tray symbolise various aspects of worship. Offerings are made to the images and are seen to be blessed. The *Om* symbol will also be prominently displayed, both inside and outside the building, to show the importance of concentration and meditation.

In all religions, the symbols used as expressions of faith are important to the religious believer. They help to give a sense of belonging and community and also contain some religious idea or teaching. Artefacts may also be regarded as special or sacred. All of this is designed to make a religious building conducive to worship.

Which religion do each of these symbols belong to? What do they represent?

Activities

3 Choose two religious traditions and create a poster showing some of the symbols found within those religions.

4 Make a list of the reasons why you think symbols are used within art and places of worship. Share your ideas with a partner and compare.

Must think about!

Music also has a long-established history in assisting worship. How do you think music compares and contrasts with religious artwork?

3.5 The purpose and place of symbolism in places of worship

The next two pages will help you to:

- understand why holy buildings are so important to religious believers
- consider why holy buildings are suitable for worship.

- **Holy buildings are a key feature in any religious tradition. Why do you think this is?**
- **What is it about a holy building that is so special?**
- **What is in them that makes them fulfil their purpose?**

Why worship in special buildings?

Why do Christians want to worship in a chapel or church? Why do Jews want to worship in a synagogue? Why do Hindus want to worship in a mandir? Here are some of the answers.

- Worship means 'to give worth to' and all religions want to worship God.
- Worshipping in a special building means that:
  - there is a special atmosphere
  - there is a sense that God is present
  - there is a focus for concentration during prayer.
- There is an opportunity to worship with others and develop a sense of community.
- Members of a family may worship together.
- It is a place used for the celebration of rites of passage, such as birth, marriage and death.
- There are opportunities for religious teaching in sermons.
- It gives people an opportunity to sing and worship in a variety of ways, other than simply praying.
- Artefacts in the building may assist the act of worship.
- It is a religious tradition.

Religious buildings are often very impressive. What symbols can you see in this image?

Activity

1 Use the bullet points above and try to rank the ideas. You may like to write each one on a piece of paper and discuss the order with a partner.

What makes a place conducive to worship?

Places of worship are designed to suit their purpose. They are often quiet places where believers are surrounded by artefacts, images and objects associated with their religion. There may be smells in the atmosphere that help worship or even sounds, such as music, that are familiar to worshippers. It is very important that a holy place is conducive to worship as this is the primary purpose of such a building.

Must think about!

Consider the outside of a religious building. What suggests it is a special or holy place? How is it designed to suit its purpose?

GradeStudio

Question

Explain two different ways in which holy buildings help worshippers.
(6 mark question, AO1)

This question tests your ability to explain religious ideas and make a link between religious faith and beliefs (AO1). Levels will be used to measure the quality of your response. A good answer will not only explain key ideas, but will provide detail and awareness of how they link to other religious beliefs and affect the life of a believer.

You could build an answer like this.

Level 1
First, make sure you show the examiner that you understand what the question is asking you. For example, 'Religious believers have holy buildings, because they suit the purpose of prayer and worship. They may have symbols in them that help believers to worship.'

Level 2
Then explain in more detail the point mentioned. For example, 'Many holy buildings have pictures, images and symbols to help believers focus and concentrate on their faith and worship. In Christianity, they may have images of Jesus on the cross to remember the sacrifice he made. They may also wear objects such as a cross or crucifix, which helps them to remember and concentrate on their faith.'

Level 3
Next, give more explanation, making sure you explain a second example or purpose. For example, 'Religious believers also claim that a holy building provides a suitable atmosphere where they can worship. They can express their faith in a quiet place where they feel close to God.'

Level 4
Finally, draw together your ideas showing a full awareness of the question. For example, 'Many holy buildings have objects that remind believers of the importance of their faith and allow them to express their faith with people who share their beliefs. It is a place where they are united and, therefore, is suitable for the purpose of worship. The atmosphere created in a holy building will be completely different from praying or worshipping alone and this is what makes these buildings special and, therefore, conducive to worship.'

Activities

2 Either visit a place of worship or find five pictures of the inside of places of worship and make a list of ways in which what can be seen suits the purpose of worship.

3 Imagine that you are being asked to design a new holy building for one religious tradition. Draw up some plans and write some notes of what you would need to take into consideration. Share your ideas with your class.

3.6 Expressing faith through pilgrimage

The next two pages will help you to:

- identify the purpose of a religious pilgrimage
- identify places that are special to religious believers.

- **Do you have a place that is special to you? Where is it?**

- **How do you feel when you go to your special place? Why is it special and what is there to make it fulfil its purpose?**

Why are special journeys a way of expressing faith?

Activity

1 In pairs, discuss the following question.

   How many religious places of pilgrimage can you identify? Can you work out which religion goes where?

What makes a journey special?

Journeys to significant places have always featured prominently in religions. Many religious leaders have completed sacred journeys, which followers have then gone on to repeat as a sign of their dedication and commitment to their faith.

Journeys may be special because:

- they are routes to places where something important happened
- someone special went that way
- you feel closer to someone there
- you can trace something back to a particular destination.

What's special about pilgrimage?

Pilgrimage is a form of religious expression and a spiritual journey. Places of pilgrimage are often associated with the founder of a religion or a particular event, or have some connection with past events in the religious tradition. All of the six main world religions have pilgrimage sites. To the followers of these faiths, these special places are sacred.

Christianity

There are no formal requirements to make a pilgrimage in Christianity. In fact, many argue that a religious life is a complete spiritual journey. Christians may choose to visit Israel to 'walk in the footsteps of Jesus' by visiting Bethlehem, Nazareth and Jerusalem. The motivation may be a sense of curiosity or wanting to be in the actual places where they believe Jesus lived and died. It may deepen their faith and they can use the pilgrimage as time for increased prayer, devotion and reflection. Many Christians may travel across England to visit the many shrines that exist.

Some Christians go on pilgrimage in expectation of a miracle. Thousands visit Lourdes in France each year; some of them are hoping to be healed. Thousands of young people from Europe visit the monastery in the small village of Taizé to pray in the Church of the Reconciliation.

In Wales, people go to Caldey Island off the coast of Tenby to visit the Cistercian monastery. Many visitors are simply tourists, spending time on a boat trip and the sandy beach of the island as part of their holiday. The men (for only men are allowed into the residential monastery buildings) may find themselves drawn to the sense of the past, the mystery, simplicity and tranquillity of the monastery, on one of the daily guided tours. Women may visit the island, but can only visit the church.

Some Christians see life as a journey or pilgrimage to God.

Judaism

Again, there is no rule stating that Jews must go on pilgrimage, but many choose to do so. They may want to visit Yad Vashem to remember the members of their families who died in the Holocaust. It is also a way of remembering past events and sharing this with new generations. Many Jews will visit Israel and, in particular, the remaining Western Wall of the Temple in Jerusalem. This is a holy city, as it is the area where Judaism was founded, and often Jews may feel a sense of peace or tranquillity at being able to trace the roots and origins of their religion.

Hinduism

The most famous centre of pilgrimage for Hindus is the city of Benares, or Varanasi, in India. It is on the banks of the River Ganges and is considered very holy. Many pilgrims will bathe there, as they believe this is a cleansing process that washes away their sins. There is no written rule that states Hindus should go on pilgrimage, but many do as they consider it part of their faith and an opportunity to deepen religious beliefs. India is the home of the religion of Hinduism and Hindus can visit places of historic importance and worship in the many temples there.

Must think about!

Why do religious believers go on journeys? What is the religious significance of a pilgrimage? Think about why religious believers consider the places to be so important. Do you think there can be non-religious pilgrimages, for example to follow sport, science, art or politics?

Activities

2   Use the information above to make a list of why religious believers go on pilgrimage. Share your ideas with a partner and add any others to your own list.

3   Find six images of different places of pilgrimage. Write a description of each one, explaining what it is in the picture that shows it is a special place.

4   In groups, choose one place of pilgrimage mentioned on these pages. Research it and produce one of the following to share with your class to help them understand the place of pilgrimage:
    ■ a poster – showing images of the place of pilgrimage
    ■ an information leaflet – explaining the importance of the place of pilgrimage and showing what happens there
    ■ a presentation to explain the place of pilgrimage to your class.

5   Individually, write a diary account as though you have visited one place of pilgrimage. Try to explain what you did, where you went, what you saw and how you felt.

3.7 Attitudes to pilgrimage

The next two pages will help you to:

- understand the importance of pilgrimage for a believer
- evaluate whether pilgrimage still has value and importance today.

- **Why do religious believers feel the need to visit a place of pilgrimage?**
- **Is it really that important?**
- **If not, does this mean that pilgrimage is out of date?**

How does pilgrimage contribute to a person's spiritual growth?

Can pilgrimage help a person's spiritual growth?

Pilgrimage is often seen as an opportunity for believers to:

- get closer to God
- understand their faith more deeply
- concentrate fully on their religion, showing a sense of commitment and dedication.

It is also a way for them to develop individually as spiritual people.

Is pilgrimage out of date?

Pilgrimage to a holy or special place can often today be viewed as being out of date. This is because it is all about a place that was important to religion many years ago and there are much more exciting places to visit today. Indeed, most of us choose to go to holiday destinations that have no religious significance. Does this mean, therefore, that pilgrimage is out of date? Many religious believers would argue that they are not as pilgrimage is a way of expressing faith, feeling closer to God and tracing the origins of the religious faith that is so important to them.

1 **a** Read the diary article from a 15-year-old boy, who went to Caldey Island with his family.

> I went to Caldey Island last summer with my family. We were in Tenby for a week and we decided to go there for a day out. My mum and girlfriend stayed on the beach, while my dad, brother and I went for a guided tour of the monastery. I thought it was going to be really boring but the guide said it was only going to be 45 minutes long. In fact it was pretty good. The guide told us some things about the monks and as we moved through the monastery it was incredibly quiet. We saw a monk's bedroom and I was surprised at how few possessions they were allowed to have. The place where they eat was set up for their evening meal and we passed a couple of monks in the cloisters. At the end of the tour we listened to the monks praying in the church; I think they were praying in Latin. I don't know why but it made the hair stand up on the back of my neck and I found it really moving. On the way back to the boat there was a big wooden crucifix set up in a little wood on the path down to the jetty. I took a photograph of it. I don't know why.

   b Answer the following questions:
- What do you think of this diary account?
- Why do you think he found the experience moving?
- Why do you think he can't explain why he took a photograph? What is the significance of this action?
- Have you ever visited a sacred place and had a similar experience?
- Do you think this is the beginnings of spiritual growth? Why or why not?

2 Using all the information on pilgrimage, make a list of the advantages and disadvantages of going on a pilgrimage. (You need to consider all the factors involved, such as costs and hazards.)

3 **a** Use the information on pilgrimage to make a bullet-point summary arguing for and against the following statement: *'Pilgrimage is out of date today.'*

   b Write an extended answer in full sentences expressing your opinion on the statement and presenting a religious view. This is how you must write in the examination.

4 Produce a mind map or summary diagram on the topic of pilgrimage.

For debate

Consider the following question.

'Do you think that humans become less spiritual as they get older?'

3.8 Expressing faith through sharing faith with others (1)

The next two pages will help you to:

- debate the issues surrounding, and value of, interfaith dialogue
- explore the role of missionaries and evangelists.

- **Religious believers agree that a fundamental part of being a religious believer is to share your faith with others. Some people, however, claim that this is imposing on others and shouldn't happen. How would you feel if someone approached you and shared their beliefs?**

- **Has this happened to you?**

Missionary, David Livingstone

Is there a purpose or value to interfaith dialogue?

The society in which we live is constantly changing. Today in Britain there are many religions. The word used to describe such a country is pluralist. There are six main world religions, and some of those who say they belong to a religion may simply do so nominally, without taking the religion seriously or showing any real interest in it. Lots of people claim to have no religious beliefs and may describe themselves as humanist or secular.

Many religious believers consider themselves to be part of a religious family. This not only involves the people in their immediate religious **community**, but may also include religious believers within the same faith from all over the world. Sharing faith and beliefs with others is natural, as they are aware that there are people everywhere who hold the same beliefs and perform the same actions as them. People who take their religion seriously, who may describe themselves as committed, may want to share their beliefs and faith with other people. **Evangelism** means spreading a faith or religion to others. Some Christians believe that they should share their faith with other people, following the example of the disciples and Jesus' teaching.

In the past, missionaries have travelled abroad from Britain, taking the Christian faith to all parts of the world. When this happened, Christianity was the principal religion in the country. The perception today, however, is that Christianity has declined as the main religion practised in Britain. As Britain has apparently become, on the one hand, a pluralist society and, on the other, a more secular society, the idea of evangelism makes many people uneasy. It is also an issue in society where interfaith dialogue is encouraged.

Jews and Hindus also think it is important to share their religion and faith. This is because they want their faith to be respected and believe their religions teach that the messages of their faith should be spread and shared. Both traditions claim that awareness of faith is important.

Is it right for people to share their faith with others?

The question needs to be considered of whether it is appropriate for others to share their faith. There is a distinction between sharing faith and imposing faith on others. Consider the arguments for and against below:

For

- It is only through the sharing of faith that some people get to hear God's message and follow their own religion.
- Sharing beliefs is part of human nature – it isn't simply a religious idea.
- As long as it is sharing and not forcing, what's the harm?
- It is interesting to learn about the faith of others and get a better understanding of their religion.
- Sharing faith with others provides a deeper understanding of their beliefs, as you can discuss them and share together in worship.
- It is important to be able to get on with other people and sharing faith ideas helps you to do this.
- Faith is an important part of someone's life and you should feel honoured that they want to share it with you.

Against

- Faith is a personal thing and should not be dealt with in public.
- Some religious believers may try to convert people.
- Some religious believers may force religion on someone who doesn't want it or who is happy with their own beliefs.
- It can be intimidating if someone you don't know stops you and starts telling you about their religion.
- It isn't necessary – if someone wants to become religious they can go and find out about the religion for themselves.

Activity

1 Write a speech trying to persuade others of your view about the following statement: *'Religion is a private matter and it is not necessary for religious believers to share it with others.'* Remember you are trying to convince them, so anticipate any counter arguments they may give by showing your awareness of them in your writing.

3.9 Expressing faith through sharing faith with others (2)

The next two pages will help you to:

- analyse and debate the purpose of the media when it comes to reporting religious events and broadcasting faith programmes
- explore how the media should be used for religious purposes.

- The media plays a very important role in our lives. It reports on events happening in the world and religion is very often at the forefront of this. However, is it ever possible for the media to be objective?

- Is the information we are given always true?

- Is there a better use of the media when looking at religious issues?

What role do the different aspects of the media play in real life?

How should the media be used for religious purposes?

How is the media currently used for religious purposes?

The media is a very powerful tool. It reports on and presents information about our world and keeps us in touch with what is going on. Sometimes, however, information concerning religion is misrepresented in the media. This raises the questions of how religion should be portrayed and whether the media could be put to better use.

Currently, the media reports on events as they happen. Some of these are related to this topic of study, and include:

- the dispute over whether religious dress or objects should be worn at schools
- places of pilgrimage – especially when events have taken a turn for the worse and there has been loss of life
- examples of celebrities or others supporting religious charities or organisations
- atrocities such as the 9/11 Twin Tower attacks and the London bombings
- disputes between religious ideas – for example, Christianity and Islamic Shar'iah Law.

Is the media always fair?

The media sometimes portrays religion in a fairly negative way. There are only a few examples of religion and the benefits it provides being portrayed or discussed in a positive way. For this reason, many religious believers are wary of the media.

Is there a better way to use the media? Could it be used as an expression of faith? There are many examples of religious television programmes and they do present religion positively. Should there be more of these? Could the media be used in a different way to promote religion and express the faith of religious believers?

Activities

1 a Collect some newspapers or look at them online. How many examples of religion can you see portrayed in them?

b Are the examples you have found mostly positive, negative or neutral? Why do you think this is?

2 Create a collage showing how the media presents religion. Find and use as many examples as possible to do with expressing faith.

3 a Make a list of any television programmes related to religion. (You may like to look at a TV guide.) Write down:
- the times these programmes are broadcast
- what you know about these programmes
- if you have ever watched any of these programmes
- if these programmes are factual or evangelical – explain why
- if the programmes are based on Christianity or other faiths.

What image is presented of religion on television generally?

b What does the information you have written down in Question 2 tell you about religion and television?

c Do you think it is possible for people to have a religious experience while watching television? Why, or why not?

d In Britain, television evangelism is not allowed on the main channels. Why do you think this is the case?

GradeStudio

Question

'The media could be used more effectively for religious purposes.' Do you agree? Give reasons or evidence for your answer, showing you have thought about more than one point of view. You must include reference to religious beliefs in your answer. *(8 mark question, AO2)*

This question tests your ability to explain differing opinions and make a link between religious faith and belief (AO2). You are also asked to include your own opinion. Levels will be used to measure the quality of your response. A good answer will not only explain key ideas, but will provide detail and awareness of how they link to other religious beliefs and affect the life of a believer.

You could build an answer like this.

Level 1
First, show the examiner you understand what the question is asking and provide your opinion. For example, 'I agree that the media could be put to better use concerning religion. There are many programmes relating to religion, but not always at the best time. Newspapers could also be used more productively.'

Level 2
Then, explain this view in more detail and offer a second view. For example, 'I think religious believers should be able to express their faith more within the media so others understand it. Religious believers would agree with me. Some religions such as Islam are often slated in the media; this is unfair as the true religion isn't represented.'

Level 3
Next, give more explanation, especially for the alternative view. For example, 'Religious believers have the same rights as everyone else to demonstrate their beliefs. It isn't fair to stop them. Many television programmes are not on at prime times or are not on prime channels so perhaps this should be looked at. Also, religious believers should be allowed to put across their faith to show their real beliefs and not present a biased view. Some people may disagree with me, as they believe the media is not the correct or appropriate place for religion.'

Level 4
Finally, draw together your ideas showing a full awareness of the question. For example, 'Some people don't want to see religion every time they open a newspaper or watch television. It is better if faith is kept personal. Many soaps and other programmes present religion in a positive way and this allows non-believers to access and understand religious views. I still agree religion should be more prominent within the media and it could be used differently, but I know that not everybody wants religion thrown at them all the time.'

3 Religious expression

Remember and Reflect

The questions in this section are based on the work you have done throughout this topic. Try to complete as many as you can.

The questions in set 1 are designed to test your factual recall and AO1 level skills (knowledge and understanding).

The questions in set 2 are more challenging, using AO2 level skills (use of evidence and reasoned argument to evaluate personal responses and differing viewpoints). The page numbers alongside most of the questions will help you to find information that might be useful for your answers. Use them to check against what you have written.

HOW CAN I EXPRESS MY FAITH?

Set 1

1	Explain what each of the following key words means. Use one sentence for each word. **a** sacred **b** evangelism **c** faith **d** pilgrimage **e** community **f** identity	**pages 66–67**
2	Give three reasons why religious believers feel it is important to support and help others.	**pages 68–69**
3	Choose two charities or organisations and explain what they do to support and help others.	**pages 68–69**
4	Give two reasons why having a religious faith may encourage someone to support and help others overcome injustice.	**pages 68–69**
5	Give two examples from three different religious traditions of items religious believers may wear to express their faith.	**pages 70–71**
6	Give three arguments for and three arguments against wearing religious items to express faith.	**pages 70–73**
7	Give three reasons why religious believers feel it is important to express their faith through what they wear.	**pages 70–73**
8	Give two examples of religious art.	**pages 74–75**
9	Give four reasons why religious believers feel it is important to worship in a holy building.	**pages 76–77**
10	Give three examples of things that make a holy building conducive to worship.	**pages 76–77**
11	Explain three things that may make a journey special.	**pages 78–79**

12 Choose two religious traditions and give an example for each of a place of pilgrimage. **pages 78–79**

13 Give three reasons to support the view that pilgrimage is out of date. **pages 78–81**

14 Give three reasons why religious believers think it is important to visit a place of pilgrimage. **pages 78–81**

15 Choose one religious tradition and one place of pilgrimage and explain what pilgrims will do there and why. **pages 78–81**

16 Do religious believers think pilgrimage is out of date? Explain their views thoroughly. **pages 78–81**

17 Give three reasons why religious believers feel it is important to share their faith with others. **pages 82–83**

18 Give three ways in which religious believers may share their faith with others. **pages 82–83**

19 Explain how the media portrays religion. **pages 84–85**

20 Give four ways in which religious believers may choose to express their faith. **pages 70–73**

21 Give three examples of objects you may find in a holy building that aid worship. **pages 76–77**

22 Give three advantages of religious believers expressing their faith. **pages 70–73**

23 Give three disadvantages of religious believers expressing their faith. **pages 70–73**

24 Explain how having a religious faith may lead to someone expressing their faith through what they wear and by going on pilgrimage. **pages 70–73, 78–81**

25 Explain religious teachings from two different religious traditions about expressing faith. **pages 70–73**

Set 2

26 Answer the following questions, giving as much detail as possible.

    a Do you believe that it is acceptable for religious believers to express their faith in whatever way they choose? Give at least two reasons to support your answer and try to include examples.

    b Do you think that pilgrimage is out of date? Explain your answer fully.

    c How do you think having a religious belief can drive someone to help and support others? Try to use religious ideas in your answer.

    d Do you think the media could be used more effectively to present religion? Explain why you think this.

27 'Faith is a private affair; there is no need for it to be shared with others.' Do you agree? Give reasons or evidence for your answer, showing that you have thought of more than one point of view. You must include reference to religious beliefs in your answer. Try to draw a table showing arguments for and against the statement, then complete your answer, making sure you use religious ideas and teachings.

28 Choose two different religious traditions. Explain their views on each of the following issues:
- believers wearing religious objects to express their faith
- why they worship in holy buildings
- why they feel they need to make their faith explicit
- how going on a pilgrimage can help them grow and develop spiritually
- what purpose they feel there is to sharing their faith with others.

GradeStudio

On these pages you will find the types of question you might encounter in the exam, along with sample answers and comments. A good understanding of this information may help you to improve the content and structure of your own answers.

You may wish to refer to the level descriptor grids in the Introduction (pages 10–11).

Question

Explain how faith is expressed through the actions of two religious charities or organisations.

(6 mark question, AO1)

This question asks you to describe how faith and action are related (AO1). Levels will be used to measure the quality of your response. A good answer will not only describe a point of view, but will also explain it in detail and show some awareness of how it links to other religious beliefs and affects the life of a believer. You will also be expected to use religious terminology and show you understand what it means.

You may wish to refer to the Level Indicator grids in the Introduction.

Student's answer

Religious believers think it is important to help and support others as this is what the religion teaches. Organisations such as Christian Aid, CAFOD and Tearfund are based on Christian principles and believe they have a duty to support and help others. **(Level 1)** All have projects to help immediately after a disaster has occurred and in the future. Faith is expressed because they are following the teachings of Jesus and Christianity, which are based on love and helping others. Jesus set this example and they are following by putting this into practice. **(Level 2)**

Comments

This student has given a detailed account showing knowledge and understanding of one religion. This response would gain Level 3, 4 marks, but in order to increase this, the student needs to offer a different charity or organisation and expand on the detail given.

Student's improved answer

Religious believers think it is important to help and support others as this is what the religion teaches. Organisations such as Christian Aid, CAFOD and Tearfund are based on Christian principles and believe they have a duty to support and help others. **(Level 1)** All have projects to help immediately after a disaster has occurred and in the future. Faith is expressed because they are following the teachings of Jesus and Christianity, which are based on love and helping others. Jesus set this example and they are following by putting this into practice. **(Level 2)**

Another religious organisation is Tzedek, which is a Jewish charity that tries to help people who need it regardless of their race or religion. They fund projects to help people regain their lives. Again, they are putting their religious teachings into practice, believing it is important to be compassionate towards others. **(Level 3)** They suggest that God made everyone equal and we should therefore offer our help to anyone who needs it. Everyone is worthy of help and care.

Faith is important to all religious believers and they teach that you should help others and support those in need. Religious charities and organisations put religious beliefs into practice and do what they can to ease the suffering of others. **(Level 4)**

Question

'There is no need for religious believers to share their faith with others.' Give two reasons why a religious believer would agree or disagree with this statement. **(1 mark question, AO2)**

This question tests your ability to present religious views and explain the reasoning behind them (AO2). Levels will be used to measure the quality of your response. A good answer will not only state a view, but will also justify that view in detail, drawing on religious beliefs and teachings.

Level 1 A simple appropriate justification of a point of view.	First, show you understand the question and state an opinion. For example, 'Religious believers claim that sharing their faith helps others to understand them.'
Level 2 An expanded justification of one point of view, which includes religious teaching OR two simple points of view.	Then justify this view by referring to religious teachings. For example, 'Many religious believers think that part of following their faith is to share it with others so they can learn from it, understand them better and perhaps even follow the faith themselves.'
Level 3 An expanded justification of one point of view, with appropriate example and/or illustration, which includes religious teaching. In addition, a second simple appropriate justification of a point of view.	Next, offer a deeper explanation. For example, 'Some religious believers may claim that, although it is important to share their faith, they should not force it on anyone and there are times when it is inappropriate to share beliefs.'
Level 4 An expanded justification of two viewpoints, incorporating the religious teaching and moral aspects at issue and their implications for the individual and the rest of society.	Finally, offer a deeper explanation of the viewpoint. For example, 'Religious believers accept that teaching and preaching is a fundamental part of their religion in order to spread the word of God, but recognise that not everybody wants to understand their faith and sometimes it may be better not to express their faith by telling and sharing with others. It can bring problems if others are not willing to listen.'

Question

'There are better ways to express your faith than by going on a pilgrimage.' Do you agree? Give reasons or evidence for your answer, showing that you have thought of more than one point of view. You must include reference to religious beliefs in your answer. **(8 mark question, AO2)**

This question tests your ability to present more than one point of view and evaluate them (AO2). Levels will be used to measure the quality of your response. A good answer will state a view and justify it in detail, drawing on religious beliefs and teachings. At the highest level, an answer will also look at the implications of these points of view for society as a whole.

Here is how you might build an answer.

Level 1	First, state an opinion, giving a reason to support your view, for example: I agree with the statement as pilgrimages today are expensive and you can just pray at home. You don't need to go anywhere else.
Level 2	Next, give examples supporting your view and refer to an alternative view linking to appropriate evidence, for example: People can wear items or tell others about their faith – they don't need to jet off across the world in order to express what they believe. Also, many religions don't have specific teachings on pilgrimage. I understand that some people may think differently. Christians may like to trace their religion and visit the places where Jesus lived.
Level 3	Then explain each view in more detail, making reference to religious teachings and practices, for example: Christians believe that pilgrimage is a good way of expressing their faith so would disagree with the statement. They think that pilgrimage is valid today. It is the ultimate commitment to travel to a holy place of importance and follow in the footsteps of Jesus. They believe it brings them closer to God and provides a necessary environment and time for them to concentrate and reflect on their faith. On the other hand, pilgrimage seems like a lot of effort for perhaps nothing in return. There are easier, less expensive ways of showing your faith, for example wearing a cross or crucifix or sharing your beliefs with others so that they gain a better understanding of the religion.
Level 4	Finally, thoroughly discuss the question, offering alternative views of the religious teachings and moral issues, for example: I still believe that pilgrimage is out of date, but I accept that many religious believers think differently. Perhaps they feel that they have made an effort to commit to their religion by going on pilgrimage and that this takes more strength than simply expressing faith in an easier way. There are other ways of showing your faith, many of which religious believers do anyway. I think many religious believers feel that putting themselves out by going on pilgrimage is a meaningful way to express their faith. They may accept that you can express your faith in many ways, but pilgrimage means making a sacrifice for your faith.

4 Authority – Religion & State

The Big Picture

- In this topic you will be addressing various ethical issues relating to authority, religion and the state.
- This topic covers three principal religions: Christianity, Islam and Buddhism.
- You will need to focus on at least two principal religions.

You will look at:

- religious practices and teachings about human rights
- the impact of authority on religion and society
- religious teachings about duty
- the purpose of punishment and religious beliefs about capital punishment
- the role of sacred texts in individuals' lives
- possible conflicts between personal beliefs, sources of religious authority and the law.

You will also think about the ways in which these beliefs affect the life and outlook of believers in today's world and different attitudes that exist towards these ideas.

What?

You will:

- develop your knowledge and understanding of religious beliefs about issues of authority, law and order in religion and society
- explain how these beliefs and religious teachings affect religious believers and how this may impact on the way they live their lives
- make links between these issues and teachings and your own ideas and opinions.

Why?

Because:

- these questions and issues are central to an understanding of human life and experience
- these are major areas of discussion and are important in the maintenance of society today
- it is important to understand a range of beliefs and teachings on some of these controversial issues
- it is impossible to live in 21st-century Britain and not have to consider these significant issues.

How?

By:

- studying and recalling information about religious teachings on these issues
- exploring the relevance and practicality of these teachings in the world today
- analysing others' points of view and comparing them to your own.

Plan to impose curfew on all teenagers

Teenagers are outraged at a new idea of introducing a curfew for all youngsters under the age of 18. It would mean that, after 9 p.m., anyone under this age not in their own homes could be prosecuted under this new law. It is thought that this measure would help to stop crime and make the streets safer.

What do you think about this idea? Do you think it would achieve the aims as explained in the article? What rights is this idea stopping? How do you think Britain might react to such a law being passed?

How might young people respond to the news in the above article?

Develop Your Knowledge

This topic is about 'Authority – Religion & State'. Read the information below, which will help you to think about the issues before you begin more detailed work.

Key information

- Every person in the world is entitled to certain rights, as detailed in the Universal Declaration of Human Rights.

- There are many reasons why religious believers consider it important to fight for justice. These include religious teachings, which often show that injustice is wrong, and the fact that some people are unable to fight for their own rights. Believers feel that they can make a difference.

- There are duties that every person should be aware of and carry out from day to day.

- There are many aims of punishment.

- People believe different crimes should merit different forms of punishment in order for justice to be achieved.

- There are many views on whether capital punishment (the death penalty) is morally right, because it involves taking a life.

- Sacred texts influence religious believers to behave or act in different ways.

- Sacred texts are viewed as important sources of authority in religious traditions, but there is debate about their interpretation and relevance in contemporary society.

- Religious leaders provide an important source of authority for religious believers.

- There is much debate about what religious believers should do when the law or personal beliefs are in conflict with sources of religious authority.

Key words

*authority right or power over others

capital punishment the death penalty; a punishment used when the most serious crimes have been committed

conscience an innate moral sense that guides actions and responses

*duty something you do because it is the accepted pattern of behaviour

*human rights something a person is entitled to because they are human

*justice where everyone has equal provisions and opportunity

offenders criminals; those who have committed an offence and done something wrong

*personal conviction something a person strongly feels or believes in

*punishment a penalty given to someone for a crime or wrong they have done

reform the idea of change, usually of a person's life or outlook

reparation the idea that something is 'paid' to compensate for what has happened

retribution revenge, to gain satisfaction that the person who committed a crime has also suffered

sacred texts holy books or sacred writings of a religion

vindication justice; the idea that the law has been upheld

*We draw attention to these key words in particular because they are the ones that appear in the WJEC specification.

- How can human rights be maintained?
- Should everyone have the same human rights?
- How can people get justice for others?
- What makes people try to get justice for others?
- How do we know our duties?
- How should we deal with offenders?
- Is it ever right to take a life?
- What influence can sacred texts have?
- How far should people follow the authority of the written word?
- Why should we obey authority?
- What if the authority is wrong?
- What if the law conflicts with religious beliefs?

For interest

This topic is all about authority, religion and the State, and it includes punishment. In ancient times, a particularly gruesome form of capital punishment was crucifixion. Death was caused by exhaustion, suffocation or heart failure. Other methods of capital punishment have included being stoned to death, burnt alive, hanged, fed alive to wild animals, ripped apart by horses pulling in opposite directions, impaled, poisoned, beheaded or drowned. A more recent method was death by using the electric chair. Today, the death penalty usually takes the form of lethal injection.

Why does the world need human beings?

Should we care about how the universe began?

Should we care about the world today?

4.1 Human rights (1)

The next two pages will help you to:

- explore what human rights are and how they can be maintained
- look at the Declaration of Human Rights and debate the issues it raises.

- **Have you ever thought about what rights you have as humans?**
- **Have you ever thought what you are entitled to or what would happen if you were denied your human rights?**

What rights should these people have?

How can human rights be maintained?

What are human rights?

Human rights are the 'basic rights and freedoms to which all humans are entitled'. All humans agree that there are certain aspects of life that everyone is entitled to.

Must think about!

At what age do you think you move from being a child to an adult? What rights do you think you have at this age and why? Make a list. What responsibilities do you think you should hold at this age?

Activity

1 a Read through the Declaration of Human Rights opposite and, with a partner, choose the ten rights that you think are the most important, ranking them from most important to least important.

  b Do you think any of the statements are out of date? Why or why not?

  c Which of the human rights do you think is the easiest and hardest to maintain? Why?

  d Do you think it is possible for everyone's human rights to be maintained? Explain your answer.

  e Read each of the statements below and then explain which human rights have not been upheld.

  - There are estimated to be over 300,000 child soldiers fighting in the world today.
  - During the last 100 years, 100 million people have died as a result of abuse, war and famine.
  - Over 40 million children live homeless on the streets in today's world.

The United Nations Universal Declaration of Human Rights lists human rights as:

DECLARATION OF HUMAN RIGHTS

1 All human beings are born free and equal in dignity and rights.
2 Everyone is entitled to all these rights and freedoms without distinction of any kind.
3 Everyone has the right to liberty and security of person.
4 There shall be no slavery.
5 There shall be no torture or cruel, degrading punishment.
6 Everyone has the right to be treated as a person before the law.
7 All are equal before the law.
8 Everyone has the right to the fundamental rights granted by law.
9 No one shall be subjected to arbitrary arrest, detention or exile.
10 Everyone is entitled in full equality to a fair and public trial.
11 Everyone is innocent until proved guilty according to law in a public trial at which they have had the right to defend themselves.
12 No one shall be subjected to interference with their privacy.
13 Everyone has the right to freedom of movement.
14 Everyone has the right to seek in other countries asylum from persecution.
15 Everyone has the right to a nationality.
16 Everyone of full age has the right to marry freely and to be equal in marriage.
17 Everyone has the right to own property.
18 Everyone has the right to freedom of thought, conscience and religion.
19 Everyone has the right to freedom of opinion and expression.
20 Everyone has the right to freedom of peaceful assembly and association.
21 Everyone has the right to take part in the government of their country, directly or through freely chosen representatives.
22 Everyone has the right to social security.
23 Everyone has the right to work, to have equal pay for equal work, a just wage and to join a trade union.
24 Everyone has the right to rest and leisure with reasonable working hours and holidays with pay.
25 Everyone has the right to an adequate standard of living.
26 Everyone has the right to education.
27 Everyone has the right to take part in the cultural life of the community.
28 Everyone is entitled to a social and international order to enjoy these rights.
29 Everyone has duties to the community.
30 The state must uphold these rights.

Should everyone have the same human rights?

Is everyone entitled to the same human rights? Should someone who has committed a horrific crime, such as murder, still be entitled to the same rights as someone who has never done anything wrong? Or do you forgo your human rights the moment you do something that takes away the human rights of someone else?

Research note

Research whether Nelson Mandela's human rights were ignored when he was imprisoned for 19 years. What human rights are ignored when dictators force people in their countries to live in poverty?

Activity

2 a Make a list of reasons for and against the following statement. Try to give at least three reasons for each view:

   'Everyone is entitled to the same rights regardless of what crimes they may have committed or whose human rights they have denied.'

   b Write your own opinion on the statement above, explaining at least two reasons for your view.

   c Why do you think human rights is such a debatable issue? Share your ideas with a partner and see if they agree with you.

4.2 Human rights (2)

The next two pages will help you to:
- explore how people try to get justice for others
- explore what motivates them.

- **Think about someone famous who has tried to fight for justice for others, such as Oscar Romero.**
- **How have they managed to do this?**
- **Why do they feel it is important to try and achieve justice?**

How can people get justice for others?
Who will stand up for human rights?

Various people have campaigned against injustice. Religious leaders have often shown the way in raising awareness of and achieving basic human rights for those who have their rights ignored. Most religious believers accept that God made everyone equal in his own image and this suggests each and every human is important.

Sacred texts

There is neither Jew nor Greek, there is neither slave nor free, there is neither male nor female; for you are all one in Christ Jesus.

Galatians 3:28

A new commandment I give to you, that you love one another – even as I have loved you, so you also love one another.

John 13:34

Oscar Romero

Read the following case study.

Case study: Oscar Romero

- Oscar Romero was born in 1917 in El Salvador. He was ordained in 1942 and is remembered for completing the Cathedral of Santo Domingo, organising the first communion and catechism, and broadcasting over the radio.
- In 1967, the region's bishops agreed to move away from trying to maintain peace and towards supporting the poor struggling for social justice. Crime and corruption were extensive and many were struggling. At the start, Romero decided not to speak out against what he saw.
- In 1977, Romero was appointed Archbishop of San Salvador. When his friend, Father Rutilio Grande, was assassinated, Romero suspended masses in the nation's churches, demanding the punishment of those responsible. Romero emerged almost immediately as an outspoken opponent of injustice and the government and a defender of the poor.
- Romero inspired many people, who crowded into the cathedral to hear him preach or who listened to him on the radio. He held meetings banned by the government, speaking out against abuse and injustice. Working against the law, he used his position to speak for those who could not do this for themselves. He was known as the 'Voice of the Voiceless'.
- Those who supported Romero were targeted with violence. On 24 March 1980, a group of unidentified gunmen entered a chapel in San Salvador, while he was celebrating mass, and shot him dead.

Activity

1 **a** Why do you think Oscar Romero was so popular and why did he stand up for the rights of others?

   b What actions did Romero take to help the poor?

   c What religious beliefs led him to take the action he did?

   d Do you think he was right to speak out, when it was against the law?

   e How was he showing Christian teaching in what he did? (Hint: Look at the sacred text quotations to help you answer this question.)

What makes people try to get justice for others?

Justice is seen as:

- helping poor people and speaking out against oppressors
- caring about others, whatever their race, colour or religion
- ensuring everyone has equal provision and opportunity
- being a peacemaker and showing the way of forgiveness
- acting on behalf of others and not being scared of the consequences.

Many religious believers have fought against injustice. Martin Luther King, Jr, Mohandas Gandhi, Oscar Romero and Muhammad are some who have put their lives at risk, and in some cases had their lives taken, to raise awareness of and fight against injustice. Many used non-violence to achieve their goals. There is a variety of reasons for this.

- They believed what was happening was wrong and unacceptable.
- They followed religious teachings supporting the idea that everyone is equal and should not be treated differently.
- They believed that God told them to stand up for others.
- Often they were fighting for people's rights, where the people involved could not stand up for themselves.
- They believed they could make a difference.

Research note

Choose one of the following who has stood up for the rights for others. Research what they did, how they achieved it and how it reflects religious teachings. Give as much detail as you can. You may want to display your findings as a case study, presentation or summary leaflet.

- Desmond Tutu (Christianity)
- Muhammad (Islam)
- Aung San Suu Kyi (Buddhism)
- Simon Wiesenthal (Judaism)

GradeStudio

Question

Explain how having a religious faith might influence someone to fight for justice for others. *(4 mark question, AO1)*

This question tests your ability to explain religious teachings and make a link between religious faith and actions (AO1). Levels will be used to measure the quality of your response. A good answer will not only explain key ideas, but will provide detail and awareness of how they link to other religious beliefs and affect the life of a believer.

You could build an answer like this.

Level 1
First, show the examiner you understand what the question is asking. For example, 'Religious believers may act in a particular way to help others overcome injustice, because of religious teachings.'

Level 2
Then explain in more detail why this is. For example, 'Religions teach that all humans are equal. Jesus gave a Commandment to love one another, which involves helping people whose human rights are being ignored.'

Level 3
Next, give more explanation, perhaps referring to case studies. For example, 'Christians believe they should always help those who are facing injustice. Oscar Romero is a key example. He gave up his life for his cause, because what was happening was unacceptable.'

Level 4
Finally, draw together your ideas showing full awareness of the question. For example, 'Believers such as Oscar Romero accept that God wants them to fight for justice, especially if others cannot stand up for themselves. The teachings and examples of believers, such as Jesus or Romero, inspire others to follow their lead and stand up for what is right.'

4.3 Duty

The next two pages will help you to:

■ identify what a duty is and how we know what our duties are
■ examine and evaluate religious teachings on the subject of duty.

■ What are some of the duties that you carry out each day?

■ What sorts of things help you to do these tasks?

■ Look at this picture; what duty does it suggest to you?

What duties do humans have on earth?

How do we know our duties?

How can duty be defined?

Duty is something that you have to **do** out of moral or legal obligation. Duty differs from rights, which are the things that individuals are entitled to **have**. Humans often recognise and carry their duties out with reference to an understood code of practice. Sometimes these codes are written down and they help us to know our duties. Some duties are related to ideas of morals – what is right and wrong. Others may be connected to the law and legal system.

We may know our duties because we are told what is expected of us. We may also know our duties because we understand what is right and wrong and how our actions have consequences and may affect others. Duties are important in society, as they ensure certain things happen. Without them, there may be disorder and chaos.

What do religions understand by duty?

In religion, there are often considered to be three types of duty:

■ to God (or the Ultimate Being)
■ to your neighbour
■ to yourself.

Christianity

■ ***Duty to God***: This is summarised in the Great Commandment, which is to love the Lord your God with all of your heart, soul, mind, and strength. (*Deuteronomy 6: 4–5; Mark 12:28–30*)

■ ***Duty to your Neighbour***: This is to love your neighbour as yourself. In the parable of the Good Samaritan, Jesus taught that anyone who needs a person's love or help is that person's neighbour. Christian duty is to treat others as you would want them to treat you.

■ ***Duty to Yourself***:
  ■ to keep your body and mind healthy
  ■ to use your talents fully
  ■ to obey the law of the state in which you are living.

Islam

■ ***Duty to God***: To submit yourself completely to the will of Allah. To maintain the Five Pillars of Islam (*shahadah, salat, zakat, sawm, hajj* – see page 23).

■ ***Duty to your Neighbour***:
  ■ to protect your neighbour's honour and help them when they are in need
  ■ to show kindness, friendship, mutual support and good treatment towards others
  ■ to share with your neighbours, even if they are non-Muslims.
  'Whosoever believes in Allah and in the Last Day, he should not harm his neighbour.' (*Hadith: Abu Huraira*)

■ ***Duty to Yourself***:
  ■ to preserve yourself both in body and in mind
  ■ to look after the world of which you are a *kalifah* (steward).

Buddhist teaching

Buddhist teaching on duty is not straightforward. The Buddha's teachings ranged from understanding (cause and effect) and developing good impressions in one's mind, to reaching full enlightenment by recognising the nature of mind.

There is no idea of 'self' in Buddhism. Buddhists believe they will attain the greatest peace and happiness through the practice of the *dharma*, that is the path or duty they choose to take. Each person is, therefore, fully responsible for himself or herself to put it into real practice. *Buddha-dharma* simply means 'Path of Awakening'. *Dharma* usually refers not just to the sayings of the Buddha, but also to the different schools of Buddhism that have developed. *Dharma* may also be seen as an ultimate and transcendent truth that is completely beyond worldly things, referring to the 'truth' or 'ultimate reality' or 'the way things are'.

Research note

Look up the Buddhist *Dharma* Wheel, or Wheel of Life, on the web. Make notes of any interesting points that you discover.

Must think about!

Do you always carry out your duties? Are there times when you know you haven't? What have been the consequences of this?

Activities

1 Think of the duties that you have to do at home. Make a list of them and share them with a partner. Do you have to do similar things?

2 What duties does mankind have within the world? Try to make a list.

3 a Choose one of the occupations below. Make a 'to do' list of five different duties that the job entails:

   Lawyer Journalist Teacher Prime Minister
   Doctor Carpenter Careworker
   Shopworker Mechanic Christian Minister

   b Exchange your list with a partner. Can you extend their list of duties? Mark which duties you think are morally binding and which are legally binding.

4 Create two separate wheels to help you recall the elements of duty from two of the three religions outlined above. Make your notes within the spokes and surrounds of the wheels.

5 Choose one of the religions being studied. Read the thought bubbles below and explain how a religious believer would act in the given situation and why.

You are a religious believer and your faith has been tested by the presence of evil and suffering in the world. What should you do and why?

You come across a person who has been attacked by a gang of youths. What should you do and why?

You see someone throwing litter on the ground. What should you do and why?

Topic 4

4.4 Punishment

- Do all similar crimes merit the same punishment?
- Can an offender really be reformed?
- Where does forgiveness fit in?

The next two pages will help you to:

- explore the difficult issue of how offenders should be dealt with – according to the offence committed
- explore the different religious viewpoints on punishment.

How should we deal with offenders?

A crime is an action considered to be wrong and punishable by law. Offenders are those who break society's agreed laws and practices. Their crimes and offences are brought before the courts, so that a fitting **punishment** or retribution can be made. Throughout history, this has been a difficult and contentious issue and, even though there are many established guidelines, each case has to be handled sensitively and carefully according to the offence committed and the circumstances that surround it.

Religions have played an important part in the development of how society deals with its offenders. Not all within the same religion may agree on how to respond with punishment.

Is locking up offenders always the answer?

What is the point of punishing someone who has committed a crime? Can you work this out from these images?

What are the aims of punishment?

- To **protect** society and the offender from each other and to make sure everyone in society is unlikely to suffer the same crime being committed again by the criminal.
- To **deter** others from committing the same offence (and the offender from doing the same thing again) because they know what will happen to them.
- To **reform** the offender and change their behaviour, so that they will change their way of life.
- To **exact retribution or revenge** on the offender or to get society's own back on the criminal. Many Christians do not accept this, because of biblical teachings: 'Never pay back evil with evil.' (*Romans 12:17*) 'Do not judge so that you are not judged.' (*Matthew 7:1*)

For interest

My object all sublime

I shall achieve in time –

To make the punishment fit the crime –

The punishment fit the crime.

W.S. Gilbert – *The Mikado*

Read this quotation from *The Mikado*. What do you think is meant by 'make the punishment fit the crime'? Do you think it is possible to make a punishment fit the crime? If so, how can this be done? If not, why not?

- To **gain reparation** for the victim. This is the idea that the criminal should compensate the victim for their loss and suffering.
- To **vindicate** society. This is to show that society and the law have authority over the criminal and that the law is being upheld and justified.
- To **ensure** a just society. This is to make sure that everyone is treated equally and fairly.

What do different religions broadly teach about punishment?

Christianity

Jesus' teachings are based on forgiveness and compassion. However, many Christians think that Jesus was setting out an ideal rather than a realistic world. Many Christians feel that punishment and forgiveness can go together. This is why they see reforming the criminal as important. They have also set up systems to make sure that punishment is fair, for example The Howard League for Penal Reform. The state of prisons was also improved in the 19th century by a Quaker, Elizabeth Fry. Nevertheless, the Christian Church has reinforced the right of the State to punish criminals, based on the verse, 'Let every person be subject to the government authorities.' (*Romans 13:1*)

Islam

Islam teaches through Shari'ah Law that no one is ever above the law, nor beneath its protection. If a wrong has taken place against a Muslim, it is considered better to forgive and be charitable. This is on the condition that refusal to take revenge does not mean loss of honour. The first thing is to reason with the wrongdoer, in the hope they will stop their offensive behaviour. Justice should always be carried out in public. This is because it is important to see that justice is done and that judges should not have the opportunity for corruption and brutality behind the scenes.

Buddhism

Buddhist teaching on punishment is that crime will always be paid for by one's future *karma*. It recognises the need to protect society from criminals and at the same time to protect criminals from creating extra bad *karma* for themselves. Buddhists believe that punishment, which sets out to hurt or destroy another person, implies that there is no other way to learn from a person's mistakes. A bad person is someone who has not yet discovered his or her potential for good.

Activities

1 **a** Look at each of the aims of punishment. Do you think that these aims are always achieved? Give an example to illustrate your answer.

   b With a partner, rank the aims of punishment in what you consider to be their order of importance. Give two reasons for the order you have chosen.

2 Look at each of the newspaper headlines below. What punishment do you feel would suit the crime committed? Explain why you think this and try to refer to the aims of punishment explained above.

Wife batters husband

Hooligan banned from town for stealing

Gang threatens terrified family

Terrorist blast – 10 confirmed dead

Drunk driver mows down toddler and keeps going

Armed robbery – innocent OAP killed

Caring husband helps long-suffering wife to die

3 Do you think it is ever really possible to forgive someone who has committed an awful crime against you? Give at least three reasons for your view. What would a religious believer argue and why?

4.5 Capital punishment

The next two pages will help you to:

- explore sensitively the issue of death as a suitable punishment for some offences
- debate whether, from a religious perspective, it is ever right to take a life.

- **Do you agree that death is a suitable punishment for certain crimes?**
- **Is it better to demand compensation than take an offender's life?**

Activity

1 Read the following statements and create a table showing whether they are 'For' or 'Against' capital punishment. Then, with a partner, rank them in order of importance.

- A LIFE for a LIFE. (This is brutal, but so is murder.)
- If life is sacred, society must not repeat the crime by paying an official executioner – an 'official murderer'.
- Life is sacred – only God gave life so only he can take it.
- Revenge is a primitive form of behaviour. It is not worthy of Christians who teach 'Love your enemy'. Jesus taught compassion not revenge.
- There is no direct statement in the Bible that forbids its use.
- It stops people taking the law into their own hands.
- In time of war, it is right to ask a person to take another's life – so why not in peace-time?
- What if an innocent person is executed? Timothy John Evans was posthumously pardoned in 1966 and George Kelly in 2003.

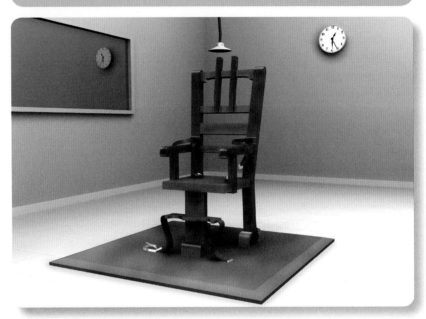

The electric chair was one method of capital punishment

Is it ever right to take a life?

This question has been debated across the world and for many centuries. Societies have long been divided over whether death is a suitable punishment for certain crimes.

What is 'capital punishment'?

Capital punishment, also known as the death penalty, is the execution of a person by the State as punishment for a crime. The Romans were famous for crucifying murderers and those found guilty of treason. In 18th-century England, over 200 crimes were punishable by death, including stealing a loaf of bread or someone's sheep! Today even treason is not punished with the dealth penalty.

Methods of execution include electrocution, lethal gas, hanging, shooting, lethal injection and decapitation. Some countries retain capital punishment for only exceptional crimes. The most frequent is murder. There are still many people who believe that the death penalty should be brought back for the most serious of crimes in society.

Throughout history, the Christian Church and other religions have accepted capital punishment as a necessary part of society. There are still many strong arguments for and against capital punishment.

Buddhism and capital punishment

There is no one Buddhist policy on capital punishment. The death penalty is inconsistent with Buddhist teaching, which places emphasis on non-violence. The Buddha did not speak about capital punishment directly, but his teachings do not seem to support physical punishment, no matter how bad the crime.

Some Buddhists argue that the death penalty is permissible, if it is used for preventative purposes. In general, Buddhist groups in secular countries such as Japan, Korea and Taiwan tend to take an anti-death penalty stance, while in Thailand, Sri Lanka and Bhutan, where Buddhism has strong political influence, the opposite is true. Almost all Buddhist groups, however, oppose the use of the death penalty as a means of retribution.

Islam and capital punishment

The intention of the Islamic law is to save lives, promote justice, and prevent corruption and tyranny. Islam on the whole accepts capital punishment, but the victim's family has the right to pardon the offender. Even though the death penalty is allowed, forgiveness is preferable. Forgiveness, together with peace, is a predominant theme in the Qur'an.

Most Muslims believe that capital punishment is a most severe sentence, but one that may be ordered by a court for crimes of suitable severity. While there may be greater punishment at the hands of God, there is also room for an earthly punishment.

Activities

2   Look up some of the suggested references below and try to work out what they are saying about capital punishment:
   Christianity – *Genesis 9:6*; *Exodus 20:13*; *Matthew 5:38–39*
   Buddhism – *The Buddha's teachings: Dhammapada 10*
   Islam – *Surah 6:151*; *Surah 5:32*

3   Choose and research one of the religious traditions' outlook on capital punishment. Design and illustrate a brochure on this subject, using some of the sacred texts to illustrate the views.

4   Answer the following examination question: *'It is never right to take a life, so capital punishment is always wrong.' Do you agree? Give reasons or evidence for your answer showing that you have thought about more than one point of view. You must include reference to religious beliefs in your answer.* (8 mark question, AO2)

GradeStudio

Question

'Murder deserves capital punishment.' Give two reasons why a religious believer might agree or disagree with this statement. *(4 mark question, AO2)*

Levels will be used to measure the quality of your response (AO2). A good answer will explain instead of simply describing why religious believers may hold different views. Try to show how it links to other beliefs.

Level 1
First, offer a simple explanation of a view. For example, refer to the fact that many religious believers disagree with the death penalty because it means taking the life of another.

Level 2
Develop your answer by referring to religious teachings or beliefs. For example, 'The Ten Commandments say, "Do not commit murder", which supports believers' claims that taking the life of another is wrong. It is viewed as murder and makes the person taking the life as guilty as the criminal being punished.'

Level 3
Ensure you give two separate reasons by showing your understanding of other evidence. For example, this could include the fact that others disagree because the criminal almost gets away with the crime, as they are not made to suffer by being imprisoned or having their human rights taken away.

Level 4
Conclude your answer by making sure that you have given sufficient explanation of your answers. For example, explain that, although there are teachings in the sacred texts that support revenge or making the criminal suffer, it is never right to take the life of another and justice can be achieved using the law system in place and other methods. Jesus used the commandment to 'love one another' and, although it is hard to do this when faced with this sort of situation, it does not make it right to carry out the death penalty.

4.6 The role of sacred texts in individuals' lives (1)

The next two pages will help you to:

- identify how sacred texts can influence someone to act in a particular way
- explore the extent of the influence sacred texts can have.

- Look at any sacred text and you will find advice and guidance on a whole range of issues. The question that must be asked, however, is what influence they have, if any?

- Also how far does their influence extend and are some of the teachings out of date today?

- Do they still have relevance to today's society?

What influence can sacred texts have?

Why do religious believers follow sacred texts?

Each world religion has its special book. They are often referred to as holy scriptures or sacred texts and they contain teachings, beliefs and religious guidance. Some religions even have more than one holy book, which religious believers will refer to when they are seeking help, advice or clarification on an issue. They are a source of authority and help believers to understand their religion better and provide help when they need it.

Sacred texts have varying degrees of influence on religious believers. For some, they provide the ultimate guidance, offering answers to difficult questions and providing advice and guidance. Sacred texts can be seen to influence how a religious believer might act or behave in given situations. A person may look for inspiration and guidance from a sacred text to ensure they are following the correct path. Many devout religious believers will base their entire lives around the teachings of their sacred text. Here are two examples.

Christianity

For Christians, the Ten Commandments are very important and they form part of a moral code for Christians to follow. They provide guidance and structure around which Christians can base their lives and actions.

For interest

The Bible is the most translated book in the world. The most commonly used word in the Bible is 'and'. 'Lord' is also a popular word and is mentioned 7,736 times!

Activity

1 Think of a book that is special to you. As a class, share your ideas about why that book is important to you and how it may have influenced you or your ideas.

WHAT SHOULD I DO?

HOW DO I KNOW WHAT IS THE RIGHT ACTION?

The Bible

Look at the Ten Commandments below:

WORSHIP ONLY ONE GOD.

DO NOT WORSHIP IDOLS.

DO NOT TAKE GOD'S NAME
IN VAIN.

KEEP THE SABBATH DAY HOLY.

HONOUR YOUR MOTHER
AND FATHER.

DO NOT COMMIT MURDER.

DO NOT COMMIT ADULTERY.

DO NOT STEAL.

DO NOT GIVE FALSE WITNESS.

DO NOT BE JEALOUS OF
YOUR NEIGHBOUR'S WIFE OR
POSSESSIONS.

Activity

2 a Why do you think the Ten Commandments are important to Christians?

b Which of the Ten Commandments do you think are easy to follow today and which are more challenging?

c How much influence do you think the Ten Commandments might have on a religious believer?

d Do you think the Ten Commandments are only relevant to religious believers? Explain why or why not, giving at least three reasons for your opinion. What do you think a religious believer would say?

e Using Christianity as an example, explain why sacred texts are important and what influence you feel teachings such as the Ten Commandments would have on a religious believer.

Islam

Muslims read part of the Qur'an every day. They believe it is important to have close contact and communication with Allah and reading his words is a method of doing this. Some Muslims will even learn the Qur'an off by heart and they are known as *hafizs*. Many Muslim children go to school at the mosque to learn about their faith, Arabic and the Qur'an. It is considered important to be able to read Arabic and the Qur'an in its original language, as Muslims believe the meaning is changed when it is translated.

The Qur'an contains guidance and advice for Muslims and, when they are facing difficult times, they can read passages that may support, comfort or assist them in their struggle.

Research note

Choose a religion other than Christianity and research what rules and teachings there are in their sacred texts. Create an information leaflet to show the influence these may have on a religious believer.

Activity

3 a How does becoming a *hafiz* show dedication and commitment to Islam?

b Why do Muslims try to learn Arabic?

c How do you think the Qur'an may influences Muslims? Try to make a list of at least five ideas.

4.7 The role of sacred texts in individuals' lives (2)

The next two pages will help you to:

- examine holy books and sacred texts as a source of authority
- determine the extent to which religious believers should follow the authority of the written word.

- **Sacred texts are important, but how much authority should they be given?**

How far should people follow the authority of the written word?

Most religious believers would argue that sacred texts are important and provide a valuable source of authority. Believers refer to them when they are challenged or need help. However, some believe they are there as a source of guidance, rather than giving the final word on all issues.

Christianity

- The main source of authority in Christianity is the Bible – considered to be the Word of God.
- Some Christians believe the Bible is literally true, while others are more liberal in attitude, claiming the Bible's teachings need to be reinterpreted for today.
- Many teachings in the Bible have a direct influence upon a Christian's daily life, as it contains rules such as the Ten Commandments.
- The Bible is used in services – a passage is read and forms part of the sermon. In many churches it is delivered from a lectern, pulpit or raised platform, showing its importance.
- In a court of law, truth statements and oaths are often taken on the Bible, demonstrating its authority.

Islam

- The Qur'an is the holy book and means 'recitation' (repeating aloud).
- Muslims believe it was received over a 20-year-period by the Prophet Muhammad in a vision from the Archangel Jibreel (Gabriel) and is Allah's final revelation.
- The Qur'an contains many rules for the behaviour expected of Muslims, but there are no specific rules on many religious and practical matters.
- It provides guidance, but rarely offers detailed accounts of historical events, instead placing emphasis on the moral significance of events.
- Hadith (meaning 'narrative') are books of the sayings and actions of Muhammad and help Muslims to follow his example (Sunnah).
- Most Muslims turn to Hadith if the Qur'an doesn't provide a clear answer.

Buddhism

- The earliest collection of Buddhist scriptures is known as the Pali Canon and is also recognised by the name 'the Tipitaka'.
- Studying the Buddhist texts is one of the most important religious activities for Buddhists, as it is through doing so that followers learn and understand their religion.
- It is believed that Buddhist texts bring about positive effects and good fortune.
- Most Buddhists recite passages when worshipping and many also chant lengthy passages, as mantras.
- Many Buddhists claim the sacred texts are more important than statues and images, so they are often kept in places of honour in shrines.
- The sacred texts contain the rules of behaviour and give examples of reports of real cases.

Are sacred texts out of date?

Today, some people would argue that sacred texts were written so long ago that they are out of date for modern society and are no longer relevant. This may be true, but many others claim that the advice and guidance given simply needs to be reinterpreted to fit within society today and, therefore, sacred texts retain their importance and authority.

Activities

1 Why do you think religious believers trust what their sacred texts tell them? Think of three reasons, then share your thoughts with a partner to see if they thought of different ideas.

2 What advantages and disadvantages are there of using sacred texts as a source of authority? Try to think of three of each.

3 Use the speech bubbles below to help you write an answer to the following question: *'Religious texts are still relevant today, even though they were written so long ago.'* Give two reasons why a religious believer might agree or disagree with the statement. (4 mark question, AO2)

Religious texts are of no value today as society has changed and we now face different issues.

Religious texts are of no use to me, as I don't read them regularly and I'm not sure I understand them.

Religious texts contain important messages from God about how religious believers should live their lives, so will always be relevant.

How do we know that the religious texts are true?

All religious texts teach good morals so will always be relevant; it doesn't matter when they were written.

I understand that we may need to reinterpret religious texts as they were written so long ago, but they will always be important to believers.

4 In pairs, look at a daily newspaper and choose five issues that appear in today's society. Choose two religions and, using the sacred texts and your own knowledge, write down what advice you think they would give to a religious believer about the issues you have identified.

5 What do you think a religious believer would do if their own beliefs were in conflict with the teachings of the religion they followed?

4.8 Examples of conflict... (1)

The next two pages will help you to:

- assess why we should obey authority
- explain examples of conflict between personal ideas and sources of religious authority.

- Look at the speech bubbles to the right. Who do you think might have said them and what sort of authority do they hold?

- Think about anyone or anything that has authority over you. Make a list of these and identify the type of authority they hold.

'Love one another as I have loved you.' This was the message Jesus was trying to pass on.

No one can tell me what to do – I have my rights and I will do whatever I want.

I promise to bring change for the better. I want to work with you and improve conditions. Vote for me!

Why should we obey authority?

What is authority?

Authority is when someone or something has the power or right to be a leader of others. Authority is something that people all over the world accept on a daily basis. People, both religious and non-religious, recognise the need to follow authority so that there is order in the world rather than chaos. But the question needs to be asked about why we should obey authority. The obvious answer may be so that we live in a harmonious world, but religions have deeper thoughts on this issue.

Christian sources of authority

- *The Bible* – As already shown, this is a key source of authority when Christians are looking for guidance or support on certain issues.
- *Religious leaders* – In the Roman Catholic Church, this is the Pope, who is believed to be Jesus' representative on earth. He is thought to be infallible in matters of spiritual interpretation. Other Church leaders such as Bishops and Archbishops, as well as Presidents in the non-Episcopal Churches, priests, vicars and ministers, are also sources of authority, as they can help religious believers to understand their faith better.

Buddhist sources of authority

- *The Buddha and his teachings* – These are believed to be an ultimate source of authority in following the example of the Buddha and gaining enlightenment.
- *Dedicated lives* – Many Buddhist monks and nuns dedicate their entire lives to studying and interpreting the Buddhist scriptures, so they can be a further source of authority for Buddhists to follow.

Islamic sources of authority

- *The Qur'an and hadith* – These are both sources of guidance for Muslims on how to act and behave in difficult situations.

- *Religious leaders* – Imams are a further source of authority in Islam, as they can advise and guide Muslims on the actions they should take. Imams are often specially chosen for the role, as they are wise and able to advise Muslims on the Qur'an and how to follow the example of Muhammad (the *Sunnah*). Other Muslim scholars are also sources of authority for the believers.

Activities

1 Why do you think that religious believers value their religious leaders so much as sources of authority?

2 Read this letter and write a response from one religious tradition explaining where they can go for help and advice. Try to include all relevant sources of authority that they could use.

Dear Sir/Madam,

My husband and I are having some difficulties at the moment. We are strong religious believers, but are having problems in our marriage and are struggling to cope with our teenage son, who is getting involved with a group of people who carry knives. We desperately need some help and guidance on what we should do and how we should deal with the issues that are troubling us.

Yours faithfully,

Richard and Amy Jones

Activities

3 Can you think of five more examples of when religious and personal beliefs may be in conflict?

4 What advice might you give to a religious believer who was struggling in this type of situation?

What if the authority of religions conflicts with personal convictions?

There are occasions when the authority of religion may conflict with the individual beliefs or **personal convictions** of religious believers. For example, if someone accepts the religious idea of the sanctity of life, but also does not agree with suffering, they may struggle to reconcile their ideas about euthanasia. There is no right or wrong answer to this type of situation. It is simply up to the individual involved to try and take the action they feel most comfortable with and follow their personal convictions. They will want to stay true to their faith, but they also would not want to go against personal beliefs that they feel strongly about. They may feel that it is down to the conscience. This means that religious believers need to consider the issue carefully and follow what they believe they can live with and what their conscience tells them is right.

What if the authority is wrong?

Religious believers accept that they have a duty to follow authority. They may disagree with the method or implementation of the authority, but they would have serious concerns about going against it. There have been cases when authority has been wrong, such as when people have been used as slaves or treated differently, because of the colour of their skin. Religious believers would raise serious concerns about such cases, arguing that the authority implementing these ideas is wrong. Again, this may come down to an individual's conscience as to what is right and many may even stand up to fight against what they see as injustices within authority.

For debate

'A religious believer must always follow their faith; otherwise there is no point in being religious.' Make a list of points for and against this statement then write a short speech illustrating your opinion. As a class, read your speeches out and take a vote as to which is the stronger side of the argument.

4.9 Examples of conflict... (2)

The next two pages will help you to:

- compare cases in which the law conflicts with religious beliefs
- explore how religious believers should act in cases where the law conflicts with religious beliefs.

- How do religious believers cope when their religious teachings conflict with what the law imposes?

- Is there a 'middle way' or is it that one of them is wrong? Religious believers are challenged to defend their teachings when they are in direct conflict with what the law states. They are forced to make a choice between what the country views as morally acceptable and what their religion is trying to promote.

What do religions say when the laws of a country conflict with religious laws?

What if the law conflicts with religious beliefs?

Religious laws v State laws?

What happens when the laws of the country are different from the laws of a religion? Which one should a person follow and how does a religious believer know how to make this decision?

There are a number of times when this dilemma can be seen and it is difficult to reconcile the conflicting ideas. For example, according to British law, it is not illegal to commit adultery (if you are old enough to have sex), but it is often viewed as being against the laws of religion. In this difficult situation, what does a religious believer do? There is no right or wrong answer, although, obviously, to ignore the rules of the country could lead to a person being prosecuted or even imprisoned. Nevertheless, a religious believer would argue that they need to be true to their faith and, perhaps, try to find some compromise, which means they remain loyal to their beliefs and religious teachings, but also stay within the limits set by the country.

Christian teaching

Read *Mark 12:13–17*. Many Christians hold the view that Jesus taught that Christians should be good citizens. They should pay any taxes that the State may legally impose and follow the rules of the country. However, Christians must also not use such laws as an excuse for not obeying the laws laid down by God.

Some Christians believe that the teachings and beliefs in the Bible were written for a very different society than today. They accept that many of them need reinterpretation in order to fit within contemporary society. They maintain, however, that the Bible is the ultimate source of authority for the Christian faith and, as such, cannot be ignored.

Buddhist teaching

Buddhists believe that their religion is all about bettering themselves and following the example of the Buddha, the *dhamma* (Buddha's teachings) and the *sangha* (the Buddhist community). They argue that the teachings are there to support and help them in their path to enlightenment and are a practical way of overcoming suffering and finding true happiness.

Buddhists argue that the laws of the country are also important and should be abided by to achieve enlightenment through the following of Buddhism. They would see little conflict between the law and Buddhist teachings.

Islamic teaching

As well as the sacred texts of the Qur'an and hadith, Muslims also follow Shari'ah Law, which is Islam's legal system. Shari'ah is a religious code for living. It is based on the Qur'an as the word of God, the example of the life of the Prophet Muhammad and *fatwas*, or rulings of Islamic scholars. It is implemented to varying degrees – from beheadings in Saudi Arabia, to the relatively liberal social customs of Malaysia.

The key issues in the United Kingdom are family law, finance and business. In practice, many Muslims turn to Shari'ah Law for guidance in many of these day-to-day matters. Sometimes, extreme punishments under Shari'ah Law are in conflict with the laws of many Western countries. These penalties may be imposed for unlawful sexual intercourse (adultery); false accusation of unlawful intercourse; the drinking of alcohol; theft; and highway robbery. Sexual offences can carry a penalty of stoning to death or flogging, while theft can be punished by cutting off a hand.

Activity

1 Consider the following dilemmas and discuss with a partner what you think a religious believer might refer to and do in the given situation. Try to discuss the views of religious believers from at least two different religious traditions.

- During war times, conscription and fighting for your country are accepted by law; however, many Christians are against violence. Should a religious believer fight?
- The law accepts that many shops can open on a Sunday. Should a Christian follow the law or the Ten Commandments, which state that the holy day should be kept as a day of rest?
- Abortion is legal in most countries, as long as it satisfies the stated conditions (two doctors' agreement, before 24 weeks... see page 50). Many religions, however, believe in the sanctity of life, which means that all life is sacred and only God can take a life. What should a religious believer do?
- Most religions teach that we do not have the right to take the life of another. How can a religious believer, therefore, cope with cases of capital punishment as this remains legal in some countries?
- Some religions, such as Islam, allow polygamy (marriage to more than one wife). What happens if the Muslims involved live in a country in which polygamy is illegal?

Must think about!

Should a person be allowed to practise what they believe to be correct even though the law of the land states otherwise? For example, Nelson Mandela's opposition to apartheid, Oscar Romero's stand on human rights, Aung San Suu Kyi's fight for democracy and Martin Luther King, Jr's leadership of the bus boycott in Montgomery, Alabama.

4 Authority – Religion & State

Remember and Reflect

The questions in this section are based on the work you have done throughout this topic. Try to complete as many as you can.

The questions in set 1 are designed to test your factual recall and AO1 level skills (knowledge and understanding).

The questions in set 2 are more challenging, using AO2 level skills (use of evidence and reasoned argument to evaluate personal responses and differing viewpoints). The page numbers alongside most of the questions will help you to find information that might be useful for your answers. Use them to check against what you have written.

Set 1

1	Explain what each of the following key words means. Use one sentence for each word.	**pages 92–93**

    a authority   **b** duty   **c** human rights
    d punishment   **e** justice   **f** personal conviction

2	Give two examples of human rights that people are entitled to.	**pages 94–95**
3	Give three ways in which someone's human rights might be ignored or threatened.	**pages 94–95**
4	Give three reasons why religious believers try to achieve justice and stand up for the human rights of others.	**pages 96–97**
5	Explain how two religious believers have tried to achieve justice for others.	**pages 96–97**
6	Explain what Christians believe about duty. (Make sure you make reference to duty to God, others and yourself.)	**pages 98–99**
7	What would Muslims or Buddhists say about duty?	**pages 98–99**
8	Explain each of the aims of punishment.	**pages 100–101**
9	Give three examples of crimes that have been committed in society today and which punishment you would consider to be appropriate and why.	**pages 100–101**
10	Write a paragraph comparing the beliefs about punishment from two religious traditions.	**pages 100–101**
11	Give three arguments for and three arguments against capital punishment (the death penalty).	**pages 102–103**
12	Would a Christian agree or disagree with capital punishment? Give at least two reasons for your answer.	**pages 102–103**
13	Why might a Muslim argue that capital punishment is acceptable?	**pages 102–103**
14	Give three ways in which sacred texts are used by religious believers.	**pages 106–107**

15 Give two reasons why we should obey authority.		pages 108–109
16 What would religious believers do if their religious teachings and beliefs conflicted with their personal opinions? Explain your answer carefully.		pages 108–109
17 What does the word 'Qur'an' mean and why is this appropriate?		pages 106–107
18 Give an example of a quote from a sacred text that a religious believer might refer to when looking at the issue of capital punishment.		pages 106–107
19 Explain one way in which a sacred text might influence a religious believer. Use examples to illustrate your answer.		pages 106–107
20 Apart from the Bible, what other sources of authority might Christians turn to when in need?		pages 106–107
21 What sources of authority might a Muslim refer to when looking for guidance?		pages 106–107
22 Give three examples of where the law might be in conflict with religious teachings.		pages 110–111
23 Explain what a religious believer might do in cases where their religious beliefs or teachings are in conflict with the law.		pages 110–111
24 How far do you think a religious believer would follow the authority of the sacred texts?		pages 110–111
25 Why might a religious believer face a dilemma if their personal beliefs do not agree completely with their religious beliefs?		pages 108–109

Set 2

26 Answer the following questions, giving as much detail as possible.
   a Do you believe that human rights can always be maintained?
      Give at least two reasons to support your answer and try to include examples.

   b Do you think that everyone should be treated the same and have the same human rights regardless of what they have done? Explain your answer fully.

   c How do you think criminals should be punished? Give examples and explain your ideas fully.

   d Do you think we should always obey authority? Explain why you think this.

27 *'Capital punishment is always wrong as it is never right to take a life.'*
Do you agree? Give reasons or evidence for your answer, showing that you have thought of more than one point of view. You must include reference to religious beliefs in your answer. Try to draw a table showing arguments for and against the statement, then complete your answer, making sure you use religious ideas and teachings.

28 Copy and complete the table below to show how a Christian, Muslim and Buddhist might respond to the statements. (Remember: not all religious believers agree on everything, so try to reflect this in your answers.)
Make sure you include reference to religious knowledge and give as many reasons for each view as possible.

Statement	What would a Christian say and why?	What would a Muslim say and why?	What would a Buddhist say and why?
Capital punishment is okay for the most severe crimes.			
Sacred texts should always be given more authority than the law of the country.			
Sacred texts have little influence on and relevance to life and society today.			
It is always important to stand up for others and try to maintain their human rights and achieve justice.			

GradeStudio

On these pages you will find the types of question you might encounter in the exam, along with sample answers and comments. A good understanding of this information may help you to improve the content and structure of your own answers.

You may wish to refer to the level descriptor grids in the Introduction (pages 10–11).

Question

'Sacred texts were written so long ago that they have no relevance in today's society.' Give two reasons why a religious believer might agree or disagree with this statement. (4 mark question, AO2)

This question tests your ability to present religious views and explain the reasoning behind them (AO2). Levels will be used to measure the quality of your response. A good answer will not only state a view, but will also justify that view in detail, drawing on religious beliefs and teachings.

In the table, the left-hand column shows what examiners are looking for at the different levels. The right-hand column shows how to build an answer.

Level 1 A simple appropriate justification of a point of view.	First, show you understand the question and state an opinion. For example, 'Religious believers would disagree as they believe sacred texts contain the word of God, which will always be relevant.'
Level 2 An expanded justification of one point of view, which includes religious teaching OR two simple points of view.	Then, justify this view by referring to religious teachings. For example, 'Sacred texts need to be reinterpreted for today's society and, although holy books were written in a different society, the same principles apply in today's society.'
Level 3 An expanded justification of one point of view, with appropriate example and/or illustration, which includes religious teaching. In addition, a second simple appropriate justification of a point of view.	Next, offer a deeper explanation. For example, 'The information in the sacred texts teaches good not bad and therefore the morals, such as the Ten Commandments in the Bible, are always relevant.'
Level 4 An expanded justification of two viewpoints, incorporating the religious teaching and moral aspects at issue and their implications for the individual and the rest of society.	Finally, offer a deeper explanation. For example, 'Holy books and sacred texts allow religious believers to trace their religion, understand its history and apply religious principles to life today. Although issues may have changed, the principles remain and offer solutions to difficult problems.'

Question

Explain two different examples of when there may be conflict between religious teachings and beliefs and the law of the country. (6 mark question, AO1)

This question tests your ability to explain religious teachings and describe what religious believers do when someone dies (AO1). Levels will be used to measure the quality of your response. A good answer will not only describe a point of view, but will also explain it in detail, and show some awareness of how it links to other religious beliefs and affects the life of a believer.

Student's answer

There are many examples of where the law and religion are in conflict. One concerns abortion. (Level 1) Christianity believes in the sanctity of life, the idea that only God can take life and, therefore, abortion is wrong. However, the law states that, within the parameters set, abortion is acceptable. (Level 2) It is difficult to reconcile the idea of abortion being legally acceptable and yet not being approved of by religious teachings and beliefs.

A second example concerns war and fighting. (Level 3) The law accepts that in times of war men should sign up to fight for their country. Some religious believers, however, are against the taking of life. (Level 3)

Comments

The student provides an accurate amount of knowledge and shows a good understanding of key religious ideas and practices. This response would gain a Level 3, 4 marks.

Two separate ideas are presented, although more detail is required, especially of the second idea. Description is important, but this question requires explanation and explicit reference to religious teachings and beliefs. In order to improve this answer, the student needs to try and expand the answer given and provide more reference to how the law and religious teachings are in conflict.

Student's improved answer

There are many examples of where the law and religion are in conflict. One concerns abortion. (Level 1) Christianity believes in the sanctity of life – the idea that only God can take life and therefore abortion is wrong. However, the law states that, within the parameters set, abortion is acceptable. (Level 2) It is difficult to reconcile the idea of abortion being legally acceptable and yet not being approved of by religious teachings and beliefs.

A second example concerns war and fighting. (Level 3) The law accepts that in times of war men should sign up to fight for their country. Some religious believers, however, are against the taking of life. (Level 3) As with abortion, life is a gift from God and humans do not have the right to take life away. (Level 4) Furthermore, many religious believers accept non-violent methods of achieving peace and justice and, therefore, would struggle to reconcile the duty to fight with their religious beliefs that violence is never the answer to solving problems. (Level 4)

ExamCafé

The examination is getting closer and it's time to think about revision. Preparation is the key to success. Exam Café will remind you of key ideas, refresh your memory of what you need to know and help you prepare for the examination.

In order to do well in this course, ensure that you understand the information thoroughly, know the style of examination questions, and are able to present, explain and evaluate information clearly.
In the next few pages you will find useful information covering:

- the examination (pages 116–117)
- tools and tips (page 118)
- exam advice (page 119)
- how to revise (pages 120–123).

Note
Think positive – exams are to enable you to show what you *can* do, not what you *can't*!

The examination

Here you will find advice on what the examination involves, the style of examination questions you can expect and what you need to remember in the examination.

What the exam involves

The examination lasts 1 hour 45 minutes. It has four questions – one on each of these topics:

- Religion and conflict (Topic 1)
- Religion and medicine (Topic 2)
- Religious expression (Topic 3)
- Authority – Religion & State (Topic 4)

At the beginning of each question is a page of visual stimuli. Don't forget to look carefully at these, as they are there to help you.

When answering questions, you will be asked to demonstrate your understanding of:

EITHER Christianity and one other principal religion

OR a Christian tradition within the broader context of Christianity.

You will be tested in two ways, using Assessment Objectives (AO) 1 and 2. You must show connections between AO1 and AO2. They are both weighted equally in the examination (50 per cent each), so it is important that you share your time and attention between each assessment.

Note
AO1 = describe, explain and analyse, using knowledge and understanding.

AO2 = use evidence and reasoned argument to express and evaluate personal responses, informed insights and differing viewpoints.

Style of examination questions

The questions have five sections (a–e), with a set number of marks available for each. These marks get higher as you progress through each topic, reflecting the difficulty of each question and the complexity of skills you are required to use.

Level descriptor grids (see pages 10–11) are used to measure your response to each question. Look carefully at these to remind yourself how the marks are allocated.

Each question has similarities, so read the following information carefully to understand how many marks are available and how you should answer each question.

a   questions always ask you to explain a key term. They are worth 2 marks.

   Example: *Explain what religious believers mean by _____.*

b   questions require you to show a link between an idea and how this may make a religious believer act. These questions are worth 4 marks.

   Example: *Explain how a religious believer might _____.*

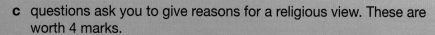

c questions ask you to give reasons for a religious view. These are worth 4 marks.

Example: *Give two reasons why a religious believer might agree or disagree with the statement _____.*

d questions require you to explain a key religious idea from two different religious traditions. These are worth 6 marks.

Example: *Explain from two religious traditions, the teaching on _____.*

e questions challenge you to agree with a given statement and provide sufficient reasons or evidence for your opinion. You are also required to demonstrate your understanding of more than one point of view, and use religious beliefs and teachings in your answer. These are worth 8 marks.

Example: *'Statement.' Do you agree? Give reasons or evidence for your answer, showing that you have thought about more than one point of view. You must include reference to religious beliefs in your answer.*

> **Note**
> In the extended writing sections, candidates are awarded marks for Quality of Written Communication (QWC). This includes:
> • legibility of writing, accuracy of spelling, punctuation and grammar, and clarity of meaning
> • appropriate style of writing for the question
> • organisation of material and use of specialist vocabulary.

What you need to remember in the examination

Each question has a 'trigger' word to help you identify the style of question. These are explained in the table below.

Question language	Meaning
'Religious believers should not be allowed to wear symbols of their faith.' **Give** two reasons why a religious believer might agree or disagree with the statement. (4 marks)	**Give** asks you to describe or state basic pieces of information or reasons for something. Make sure you are clear and concise in your response.
Explain from two different religious traditions, the teachings about taking part in a war. (6 marks)	**Explain** asks you to do more than simply describe; it means 'set out reasons for'. It requires some comment on facts or beliefs you describe. Don't just list ideas; give examples to show your understanding.
'Euthanasia is always wrong.' **Do you agree?** Give reasons for your answer, showing you have thought about more than one point of view. You must include reference to religious beliefs in your answer. (8 marks)	**Do you agree?** uses evaluation skills and requires you to consider a statement and present differing points of view. Make sure you provide: • your opinion with reasons • alternative views with supporting evidence • reference to religious beliefs and teachings • awareness of how someone's beliefs may affect their view and actions on an issue.

Remember, when answering questions:

■ read each question carefully (what information is it asking you to focus on?)
■ look at how many marks are available (what were the level descriptors?)
■ note the 'trigger' word that explains how you should answer the question (what is the question asking you to do?).

Remember, good preparation will build your confidence. Above all, don't panic! Keep reading this section for more tips and advice...

ExamCafé

Tools and tips

This section will give you advice on how to plan your revision, learn the information thoroughly, and avoid the common mistakes and errors made in examinations.

Planning your revision

It is important you have a clear understanding of the topics you have studied. This means knowing and being able to fully explain key words and ideas, which in turn means there is basic factual learning to be done! Here are some questions to get you thinking.

This will help you to structure your revision and cover all the topics thoroughly.

☐ Have I created a realistic timetable for my revision that I will stick to?

☐ Will the conditions around me help me to revise, rather than distract me?

Ensure you are sitting somewhere where you can concentrate without distractions.

You will need these in case you want to check anything.

☐ Are all my notes and materials close by?

☐ Am I regularly going through the information I need to learn?

When you have done some revision have a break, then return to it and see how much you can remember.

Resting your brain is important and will give you time to process the information you have revised!

☐ Am I taking regular breaks?

Methods of revising

- Use revision note cards/memory cards. Use pictures and words to help prompt key ideas.
- Use large concept maps of ideas. Stick them up where you will regularly see the information.
- Colour code your notes. This helps to identify key words/ideas.
- Ask someone to test you. Checking your learning is very important.
- Repeat information aloud to yourself. Saying things aloud sometimes helps us to remember things.
- Record your notes and play them back. Listening to the information regularly will help you to consolidate it.
- Use the Internet for background information. There is plenty of help available.
- Use the CD-ROM exam help. This will focus your revision.
- Write out some practice questions and test yourself. Use the level descriptors (pages 10 11) to check and mark your answers.
- Practise examination-style questions. Try to identify where your answers can be improved, and provide yourself with a checklist of information to include.

Note
We all learn things differently, so find a revision technique that suits you. There are plenty to choose from!

Avoiding common mistakes and errors

You are more likely to avoid making common mistakes and errors if you know what they are in the first place! This list gives a typical selection.

Misreading the question. Many candidates misread questions or fail to read them thoroughly. So they answer the question they *think* has been asked rather than the one that has *actually* been asked. Candidates recognise a key word and fail to answer the question in context.

Giving simple descriptions without full explanations. Candidates often fail to recognise the difference between describing and explaining. An explanation involves providing detail about what has been described. It requires some comment from candidates on the topic being discussed.

Not including specific religious teachings. In all questions it is vital that reference is made to religious teachings, beliefs and ideas. Without this, it is very difficult to achieve the higher descriptive levels in answers.

Providing generic answers. Many candidates are unsure of specific religious information, so they provide a general answer. It is important that answers reflect specific knowledge and understanding. Religious vocabulary will also help to demonstrate better understanding of religious ideas.

Writing too much or waffling. Waffling in exams is a key mistake. Many candidates write more than the space provided on the examination paper, which means time is wasted that could be given to other questions. Also, mindless waffle that does not answer the question is a waste of valuable examination time.

Only giving *your* opinion on an issue. Evaluation questions clearly state that reference should be made to alternative views. Religious teachings should also be included.

Exam advice

Take a look at the notes below, then, as a starting point to success, familiarise yourself with the topics and key questions covered in the exam.

Note

Exam conditions put us under pressure to remember information and answer questions in a time limit. So it is very easy to make mistakes. Remember, an exam is a test of what you can do, not what you can't do.

- Make sure you are clear about which religious tradition you are explaining the ideas for. Many candidates accidentally mix up ideas. (Venn diagrams may help you to compare and contrast ideas.)
- Try to be specific in your answer and give detailed responses. Explain and discuss ideas rather than just present information. (Make a checklist of beliefs and teachings you should try to include.)
- Some of the issues are sensitive or highly controversial. Try to show you understand this in your answers.
- Make sure you look at and understand how questions are marked. Your responses will be marked according to level descriptors, so you must be careful to ensure you know which questions are AO1 and which are AO2. Look carefully at the number of marks available.
- Attempt as many past paper questions as you can. This will help you to cover several possible question types and will help you to understand how to answer them. Make sure you ask a teacher to mark them or check your answers against the mark scheme.

Good luck!

Topics of study

Topic of study   1 Religion and conflict
Key questions
How can peace be made and kept?
How can good relationships be developed between people?
How can communities work together?
How can different religions support peace by talking to each other?
Why do the innocent suffer?
How can those suffering be helped?
Is forgiveness possible?
How important is forgiveness?
How important is it to forgive?
How do people learn to forgive?
Is it ever right to fight?
How can war/conflict be avoided?
Can a war ever be 'just'?
How can non-violent protest be used?

Topic of study   2 Religion and medicine
Key questions
Why is life so special?
Should people have free will to make life/death decisions?
What are the moral issues a couple must consider in life and death decisions?
How do doctors make ethical decisions?
What are the dilemmas faced by scientific advancements?
How does a religion help or hinder people making decisions?
Does the decision depend on the situation?
What are the rights of the unborn child?
Whose choice should it be concerning the issue of abortion?
Whose life is it anyway?
Is it ever right to end someone's life?
Is it right to spend so much money on IVF when people are starving in the world?

Topic of study   3 Religious expression
Key questions
Can a religion give a purpose in life?
Why do people support others?
How can a belief drive actions?
How can faith be expressed through what people wear?
Do religious believers need to make their faith explicit?
How can art express one's faith?
Why worship in special buildings?
What makes a place conducive to worship?
What makes a journey special?
Can pilgrimage help a person's spiritual growth?
Is pilgrimage out of date?
Is there a purpose or value to interfaith dialogue?
Is it right for people to share their faith with others?
How should the media be used for religious purposes?

Topic of study   4 Authority – Religion & State
Key questions
How can human rights be maintained?
Should everyone have the same human rights?
How can people get justice for others?
What makes people try to get justice for others?
How do we know our duties?
How should we deal with offenders?
Is it ever right to take a life?
What influence can sacred texts have?
How far should people follow authority of the written word?
Why should we obey authority?
What if the authority is wrong?
What if the law conflicts with religious beliefs?

ExamCafé

Let's revise... Religion and conflict
Checklist for Topic 1
In order to do well in this topic you will need to:

- [ ] be able to explain religious ideas about peace – for example, how peace can actually be achieved and how communities can work together to maintain peace once it is achieved

- [ ] be able to explain the nature and purpose of suffering and identify what support is available for those who do suffer – for example, exploring why people suffer, the different forms suffering can take and what action can be taken to put an end to or manage suffering

- [ ] be able to discuss the issue of forgiveness and reconciliation – for example, the importance of forgiveness and the study of individuals or groups who campaign and work to achieve forgiveness and reconcile people as a community

- [ ] assess attitudes towards war and conflict – for example, whether it is ever right to fight and if any religious or non-religious war can ever truly be justified by its purpose

- [ ] explain religious beliefs, teachings and attitudes towards non-violent protest – for example, assessing how methods of non-violent protest can be used and evaluating their success

- [ ] explain why different people hold different beliefs and their evidence for their views – for example, why religious believers behave and act in different ways and how their actions are related to their beliefs

- [ ] be able to explain your own views on the subjects contained in this topic and support your opinions with relevant evidence – for example, what you think about each of the subjects studied and the evidence you can present to support your opinions.

Now it's your turn
You have received lots of advice and tips about revision for this topic. Below are some activities you might like to try.

Activities

1 Create flashcards with each of the key terms for this unit on one side and their meanings on the reverse. Test your knowledge of them by laying them out and checking if you know the definitions.

2 Make a list of examples of suffering and reasons why people suffer.

3 Create a table showing reasons for and against the statement: 'It is never right to fight.'

4 Give two reasons for each of the views below.
   - *Forgiveness is important.*
   - *It is never possible to truly forgive.*
   - *Peace is an unreachable idea.*

5 Make a quiz on this topic and give it to a partner, then mark their answers.

6 Produce some revision note cards for this topic. With a partner, test each other on your knowledge of key terms and ideas.

Let's revise... Religion and medicine

Revision checklist for Topic 2

In order to do well in this topic you will need to:

- ☐ be able to explain why life is so special and the considerations that need to be taken into account in life and death situations – for example, why religions consider life to be sacred and whether humans should have free will to make life and death decisions
- ☐ be able to explain what position a doctor must take in ethical choices and how religion can contribute in moral dilemmas – for example, looking at the doctors' Hippocratic Oath and the problems that arise when trying to make difficult ethical decisions
- ☐ be able to explain in detail the issues raised by the topic of abortion and arguments for and against abortion – for example, whether the mother or unborn child's right to life is greater, who should make the decision on when life begins and whether abortion is ever justifiable
- ☐ assess whether ethical decisions should depend on any given situation rather than a 'one rule fits all' approach – for example, whether we should take into account the individual circumstances of each case or whether all ethical decisions should be made according to set rules
- ☐ explain religious beliefs and teachings about euthanasia and whether it is ever right to take the life of another – for example, whether it is ever justifiable to help someone die to end their extreme suffering and what religion says about euthanasia
- ☐ explore the issue of IVF and determine whether it is justifiable to allow this when there are people in the world without basic needs, such as food – for example, whether we can allow expensive treatments such as IVF when there are people starving in the world
- ☐ explain why different people hold different beliefs and the evidence for their views – for example, why religious believers behave and act in different ways and how their actions are related to their beliefs
- ☐ be able to explain your own views on the subjects contained in this topic and support your opinions with relevant evidence – for example, what you think about each of the areas studied and the evidence you can present to support your opinions.

Now it's your turn

You have received lots of advice and tips about revision for this topic. Below are some activities you might like to try.

Activities

1 Make a list of all the key terms for this unit and try to write down the meaning of each one. Check your answers against the information in the student book.

2 Create a crossword on this unit for other members of your class to complete.

3 Bullet point your opinion on the following statements. Then bullet point religious views from two religious traditions. Try to include religious teachings and beliefs as evidence of their views.
– *Euthanasia is always wrong.*

– *The sanctity of life is always the primary consideration when making ethical decisions.*
– *The rights of the unborn child should always be considered in cases of abortion.*

4 Create a table showing the arguments for and against abortion and euthanasia.

5 Practise some answers to examination questions. Use the level grids (pages 10–11) to mark your answers, then try to improve them if necessary.

6 Write down ten questions about this topic, then swap with a partner and see if you can answer theirs.

ExamCafé

Let's revise... Religious expression

Revision checklist for Topic 3

In order to do well in this topic you will need to:

☐ be able to explain in detail how religious charities and organisations work to support others – for example, how beliefs can direct actions and what people do to support others

☐ assess whether religious believers have to make their faith explicit and how faith can be expressed through what religious believers wear – for example, what believers from different religions wear to express their faith and whether they should be allowed to do so

☐ be able to explain how faith is expressed through symbols in places of worship – for example, looking at themes in religious art and why believers feel it is important to worship in a place of religious significance

☐ be able to give examples of how faith is expressed through special journeys and pilgrimages – for example, explaining how pilgrimage can help believers to develop spiritually and whether pilgrimage continues to have relevance in today's society

☐ explore how religious faith is expressed through sharing faith with others – for example, whether different faiths should share their ideas and how the media can be used positively and negatively to assist in communication

☐ explain why different people hold different beliefs and their evidence for their views – for example, why religious believers behave and act in different ways, and how their actions are related to their beliefs

☐ be able to explain your own views on the issues contained in this topic and support your opinions with relevant evidence – for example, what you think about each of the issues studied and the evidence you can present to support your opinions.

Now it's your turn

You have received lots of advice and tips about revision for this topic. Below are some activities you might like to try.

Activities

1 Write the key terms and definitions on pieces of paper. With a partner, see if you can match them up correctly.

2 Produce an ideas map showing how different religious traditions express their faith. Share your ideas with others in the room and see if you had the same thoughts.

3 Explain two reasons for each of the following statements, making sure you refer to religious teachings.

 – *Religious believers should be allowed to express their faith any way they want.*
 – *Religion gives people a purpose in life and teaches the importance of helping others.*

 – *Pilgrimage is still valuable to society today.*

4 Create a table showing the reasons for and against religious believers sharing their faiths with each other. Colour code your arguments to show how strong they are.

5 Write three examination questions. Then write a mark scheme for each question, using the appropriate levels. Swap your questions with a partner and write an answer. Using your mark schemes, mark the answers.

6 Write a speech giving your view about whether worshipping in special buildings is necessary. Then try to give some opposing arguments, referring to religious teachings in your answer.

Let's revise... Authority – Religion & State

Revision checklist for Topic 4

In order to do well in this topic you will need to

☐ be able to explain how individuals have campaigned for human rights – for example, why some people think it is important to fight for human rights, looking at specific individuals and their actions in their fight for human rights

☐ be able to give examples of what duties humans have and how we know we ought to perform them – for example, why we should behave in a particular way and what the consequences are if we fail to do so

☐ be able to explore the aims and purpose of punishment – for example, what punishment is suitable for the crime committed and whether punishment is effective

☐ explain forms of capital punishment and assess whether it is justified – for example, whether humans have the right to take the life of another who has committed a serious crime

☐ explore the role of sacred texts and holy books as a source of authority – for example, whether sacred texts are still influential and how much authority they should be given in today's society

☐ present examples of conflict between personal convictions and the State – for example, whose authority takes precedence and what happens if there is conflict between sources of authority

☐ explain why different people hold different beliefs and their evidence for their views – for example, why religious believers behave and act in different ways, and how their actions relate to their beliefs

☐ be able to explain your own views on the issues contained in this topic and support your opinions with relevant evidence – for example, what you think about each of the subjects studied, and what evidence you can present to support your opinions.

Now it's your turn

You have received lots of advice and tips about revision for this topic. Below are some activities you might like to try.

Activities

1 Write a key word quiz for a partner to complete.

2 Make a list of the aims and purposes of punishment.

3 Give your opinion on the following statements. Then try to explain two religious views on them, including sufficient reference to religious teachings to support each view.

– *Those who commit crimes should have their human rights denied.*

– *Capital punishment can never be justified.*

– *Holy books are out of date and no use as a source of authority today.*

4 Choose an examination question from this topic and make a checklist of ideas that need to be included.

5 Make some revision notes for this topic – either concept maps or revision cards.

6 Create a quiz on this topic for a partner to complete and then mark their answers.

Glossary

abortion ending a pregnancy by removing an embryo or foetus from the womb; this results in the death of the embryo or foetus

adultery sexual intercourse between a married person and someone who is not their legal partner

ahimsa in Buddhism, the duty of non-violence towards all living things

authority right or power over others

blood transfusion the transfer of blood to another person

capital punishment the death penalty, a punishment used when the most serious crimes have been committed

cloning the process of making an identical copy of something (the problem is that any defects, illnesses, etc. are also copied)

community group of people who are joined together because they share something in common

conflict clashes and breakdowns of relationships

conscience an innate moral sense that guides actions and responses

conscientious objectors people who, on religious, moral or ethical grounds, refuse to fight in a war

crucifix a figure or picture of Jesus fixed to the cross

duty something you do because it is the accepted pattern of behaviour

euthanasia literally means 'good death'; helping someone to die in a painless manner

evangelism spreading a faith or religion to others

faith trust or confidence

forgiveness ceasing to blame someone for something they have done wrong

free will the belief that nothing is determined

genetic engineering altering the structure and characteristic of a gene; this is done for many reasons, such as to improve the quality of crops and foods

guru a spiritual leader

hadith the sayings and actions of the Prophet Muhammad

Hippocratic Oath a special promise made by those working in medicine to do their best to preserve a life

Holocaust the mass murder of Jews by the Nazis during the Second World War

hospice a home for the care of people who are terminally ill

human rights something a person is entitled to because they are human

humanists people whose outlook attaches more importance to human than divine matters

identity sense of who you are in terms of attitudes, character and personality

imam in Islam, a person who leads prayers

injustice when things are unfair and human rights are denied; everything is not equal

interfaith community a community that makes possible religious respect and dialogue between and among all people

interfaith dialogue exploring common grounds between different faith groups

IVF stands for 'in vitro fertilisation'; this is when a sperm and egg are fertilised outside the womb

jihad an Islamic term for 'struggle'

just war a war undertaken to protect the innocent or those being violated and to restore justice and peace

justice where everyone has equal provisions and opportunity

long-term aid help that is given that is intended to last long term, such as giving people help to become self-sufficient

mandir a Hindu temple

medical ethics the moral principles that affect medical issues and practice

missionaries those involved in religious mission work

moral evil suffering caused by other humans, for example the Holocaust

natural evil suffering not caused by someone or something, for example volcanic eruptions or tsunami

nirvana the ending of material existence; the best state that it is possible to reach

non-violent protest showing disapproval without damaging property or causing any threat

offenders criminals; those who have committed an offence and done something wrong

original sin the traditional Christian doctrine that, because of the Fall of Man, every human being inherits a 'flawed' or 'tainted' nature in need of rebirth and with a natural tendency to sin; it is also known as the 'Sin of Adam'

pacifism the belief that any form of violence or war is unacceptable

palliative care treatment of pain and discomfort to make life easier for people who are terminally ill

personal conviction something a person strongly feels or believes in

pilgrimage form of spiritual adventure

pluralist describes a country where there are many religions

punishment a penalty given to someone for a crime or wrong they have done

quality of life the extent to which life is meaningful and pleasurable

reconciliation bringing harmony to a situation of disagreement and discord

reform the idea of change, usually of a person's life or outlook

reparation the idea that something is 'paid' to compensate for what has happened

retribution revenge, to gain satisfaction that the person who committed a crime has also suffered

rosary a string of beads used by Roman Catholics to guide their prayers

sacred revered or respected above other things

sacred texts holy books or sacred writings of a religion

sanctity of life life is precious and utterly priceless

secular claiming to have no religious beliefs

short-term aid help given to those who need it immediately after a disaster to ensure they can survive

suffering patience, endurance: the bearing of (or undergoing) pain or distress

surah a chapter of the Qur'an

surrogacy an arrangement where one woman carries a child for another couple

symbolism representation of an idea through actions or images

synagogue a Jewish place of worship

vindication justice; the idea that the law has been upheld

Index

Key words from the beginning of each topic are shown in **bold** type, and the page number that is also in bold will take you to a definition of the word.